ZERO TOLERANCE AND OTHER PLAYS

MW01252992

Social Fictions Series

Series Editor
Patricia Leavy
USA

The *Social Fictions* series emerges out of the arts-based research movement. The series includes full-length fiction books that are informed by social research but written in a literary/artistic form (novels, plays, and short story collections). Believing there is much to learn through fiction, the series only includes works written entirely in the literary medium adapted. Each book includes an academic introduction that explains the research and teaching that informs the book as well as how the book can be used in college courses. The books are underscored with social science or other scholarly perspectives and intended to be relevant to the lives of college students—to tap into important issues in the unique ways that artistic or literary forms can.

Please email queries to pleavy7@aol.com

International Editorial Advisory Board

Carl Bagley, University of Durham, UK
Anna Banks, University of Idaho, USA
Carolyn Ellis, University of South Florida, USA
Rita Irwin, University of British Columbia, Canada
J. Gary Knowles, University of Toronto, Canada
Laurel Richardson, The Ohio State University (Emeritus), USA

Zero Tolerance and Other Plays

*Disrupting Xenophobia, Racism and Homophobia
in School*

By

Tara Goldstein
Ontario Institute for Studies in Education, University of Toronto, Canada

SENSE PUBLISHERS
ROTTERDAM / BOSTON / TAIPEI

A C.I.P. record for this book is available from the Library of Congress.

ISBN 978-94-6209-450-5 (paperback)
ISBN 978-94-6209-451-2 (hardback)
ISBN 978-94-6209-452-9 (e-book)

Published by: Sense Publishers,
P.O. Box 21858, 3001 AW Rotterdam, The Netherlands
https://www.sensepublishers.com/

Printed on acid-free paper

All rights reserved © 2013 Sense Publishers

No part of this work may be reproduced, stored in a retrieval system, or transmitted in any form or by any means, electronic, mechanical, photocopying, microfilming, recording or otherwise, without written permission from the Publisher, with the exception of any material supplied specifically for the purpose of being entered and executed on a computer system, for exclusive use by the purchaser of the work.

TABLE OF CONTENTS

TABLE OF CONTENTS

INTRODUCTION

This book presents three research-based plays on the themes of racism, xenophobia and homophobia that can be used by teachers, teacher educators and others who work with youth in schools. The plays will also interest university instructors who are teaching courses in anthropology, cultural studies, diaspora studies, equity studies, immigration studies, sexual diversity studies, sociology, and women's studies as a resource to provoke reflection and discussion about the experiences of marginalized families in North America. In creating the plays, I worked with the approaches of performed ethnography and research-informed theatre, which has allowed for rich readings, performances and discussions of all three plays.

The world of performed ethnography and research-informed theatre attracts a variety of people from different backgrounds. This includes playwrights who are looking for ways to investigate a particular aspect of the human condition or a particular moment of human history that can be dramatized and performed for an audience. This also includes academic researchers working in a range of fields – including anthropology, sociology, psychology, education, health care, women's studies, justice studies, ethnic studies, cultural studies, political science, journalism, human communication and performance studies – seeking an effective way of sharing their research findings with audiences both within and outside of the academy.[1] I am both: a playwright and an academic.

I wrote my first research-informed play, *Hong Kong, Canada*,[2] in the late 1990s as an early-mid-career academic who had been formally trained in an anthropological research method known as critical ethnography. While the work of ethnography is to describe a culture or a way of life from the point of view of those who are living it, critical ethnography attempts to get beyond people's daily assimilated experiences to expose the ways in which institutional power impacts on everyday life.

For the first twelve years of my academic life, I engaged in traditional critical ethnographic research in the field of education. I undertook two critical ethnographic studies on the subject of teaching and learning in multilingual, multicultural, and multiracial classrooms.[3] However, by the late nineties, I began to experiment with transforming the findings of my ethnographic research into play scripts that could be read aloud by a group of participants or performed before audiences. I called my work 'performed ethnography', and soon learned that what I was writing was also known as 'performance ethnography' and 'ethnodrama'.

The term 'performance ethnography' has been used by American sociologist, Norman Denzin (2003) to refer to performances that ethnographers stage from their interviews and observation field notes. The term 'ethnodrama' has been used by American researcher and theatre artist, Johnny Saldaña. He describes *ethnodrama* as a dramatic script that consists of significant selections of narrative that have been collected through interviews, observation field notes, journal entries, diaries, media articles and court proceedings (Saldaña, 2005). For Saldaña, ethnodrama is different from *ethnotheatre*, which uses the traditional craft and artistic techniques of theatre production to mount a live performance event of research participants' experiences and/or a researcher's interpretation of data. In ethnotheatre, the fieldwork conducted by a researcher is preparation for a theatrical production.

Although the terms 'performance ethnography', 'ethnodrama' and 'ethnotheatre' are widely used in social science arts-based research conversations, I still prefer my own term *performed ethnography* because it suggests that I have deliberately written my ethnographies in the form of a play script so that they can be read out collectively, performed and discussed by others.

THE PLAYS

Zero Tolerance (2008)

In May 2007, 15 year-old high school student, Jordan Manners was shot and killed in the hallway of his Toronto school. One month later, the Toronto District School Board commissioned an investigation into school safety, which resulted in a four-volume 595-page report entitled *The Road to Health*. The report was released to the public on

January 10, 2008, at a press conference convened by the Director of the Toronto District School Board.

One month after that, in February 2008, I adapted *The Road to Health* into a 30-minute performance script to provoke discussion about the investigative report among teacher candidates and teacher educators in Toronto. The script, directed by MA student and theatre artist, Jocelyn Wickett, was performed in September 2008, for 500 teacher candidates at the Ontario Institute for Studies in Education (OISE)'s annual Safe Schools Conference.

Adapting the four-volume report into a 30-minute performance piece for teacher candidates was challenging. When I began writing the script, the report had already begun to be discussed in the local media and in neighbourhood community forums. One of my first adaptation decisions was to include public responses to the report, as well as excerpts from the report itself, in the performance script.

A second early adaptation decision was imagining the audience that would be engaging with the performance script. OISE's annual Safe Schools Conference for initial teacher education students was an ideal venue for a performance of *The Road to Health*, so I decided to write the script for an audience of teacher candidates and their teacher educators, who were my colleagues at OISE. These two early decisions provided me with several characters for the script: a media reporter and a group of five new teachers.

A third early decision was to write myself into the script, by giving myself the role of narrator. I made this decision because I felt it was important to remind the audience that the performance they were about to see was an *interpretation* of the report, only one of many that had been made by a number of educators, community leaders, government officials and the media since the report had been released. As contemporary researchers have been writing for decades now, writing up research data is an interpretative, subjective, value-laden project (see for example, Behar, 1995; Clifford, 1983; Clifford & Marcus, 1986; Goldstein, 2008). I wanted my audience to remember that the performance was inventing truths about the meaning of the report at the same time as it was attempting to represent truths contained in the report. I used the notion of 'story' to do this. The opening monologue sets up the performance as a story that Tara Goldstein, a playwright and teacher educator from OISE, has written based on her reading and understanding of *The Road to Health*.

One of the most difficult tasks of adapting the report for the stage was deciding which aspects of the report to share in the performance. As can be seen from the title of the play, I decided to tell a story about an approach to school safety known as 'zero tolerance'. The story of zero tolerance is only one of the stories told in the report however, I felt the story of zero tolerance was important because it provided my audience with an understanding of a particular approach to school violence that has not made schools any safer or healthier.

The executive summary of *The Road to Health* begins with a somber reminder of why an investigation into school safety within Toronto schools is necessary.

> It is all too easy to forget why we are here: Jordan Manners was five days beyond his fifteenth birthday when he died on May 23, 2007 in the hallway of C.W. Jefferys C.I. Secondary School ("C.W. Jefferys") as a result of a bullet wound to the chest. ... [we have] carefully laid out the last moments of Jordan's life as he lay dying in the hallway of C.W. Jefferys to ensure that it is all very real. It is certainly real for those who personally experienced Jordan's loss and it now should be real for all who claim an interest in the subject matter of this Report: the safety of youth. (p. 1)

In adapting the report for the stage, I agreed with the authors that Jordan Manners' death needed to be made real for new teachers whose work will involve working towards safer and healthier schools in Toronto. So, like the authors, I also decided to tell the story of the last moments of Jordan's life after being shot in the hallway of his school. I then decided to have the new teacher characters recount the story of how Jordan was shot and added their responses to the telling of the horrific story. I also added the imagined responses of the high school students who went to school with Jordan. Both the performers and audience members reported that the story of the shooting of Jordan Manners was the most emotionally powerful part of the performance.

To end the play, I gave a final monologue to the narrator Tara Goldstein. The monologue closed with the question, "How can we do our part at OISE to work against another shooting at a Toronto school?" Each of the five new teachers repeats the same question asking, "How can we do our part?" The call to action for new teachers and teacher educators at OISE to do their part was intended to inspire the audience to take full advantage of the opportunities to learn more about safe school issues and safe school practices at the workshops that immediately followed the performance. Such a call is typical of performed ethnography, which strives to promote dialogue and cultivate new understandings around important social issues (Denzin, 2003; Leavy, 2009).

Lost Daughter (2008)

Lost Daughter is a historical drama that is based on interviews, photos and written documentation about racial/ethnic tensions between Jews and non-Jews in Toronto, Canada, during the summer 1933. It was a summer of intense heat and widespread unemployment. It was also a summer when Gentile youth wore swastika badges to keep the city's Jews out of Toronto's public parks and off its beaches.

Imagined as a kind of a sequel to Shakespeare's *The Merchant of Venice*, a play that is taught in English-speaking secondary schools worldwide, *Lost Daughter* explores what happens to Shylock's daughter, Jessica after Shakespeare's play has ended. I had wanted to write *Lost Daughter* ever since I was a high school student myself, in another Canadian city, the city of Montreal. *The Merchant of Venice* was required reading in our grade nine English class and I was chosen to read aloud the part of Shylock. The year was 1971, and the majority of the students in the English class, like me, were of Jewish background. Yet, the binary of Christian forgiveness (most explicitly expressed by Portia's "quality of mercy" speech) and Jewish revenge (most explicitly symbolized by Shylock's desire for a pound of flesh) in the play was never discussed. At the end of our play reading, the Jewish students in the class were left with the uncomfortable suggestion that Christians were merciful, and Jews, who were vengeful, needed to be punished.

This message contradicted everything I had learned about the deep, rich tradition of Jewish forgiveness, good deeds, and repentance. It also reproduced the kind of anti-Semitism that had been used to justify the extermination of six million Jews in Europe during the Second World War. In our grade nine English class, there were children of Holocaust survivors. What we all needed to learn was how to critique Shakespeare's binary of Christian mercy and Jewish revenge, and how to respond to the xenophobic and anti-Semitic ideas and anti-Semitic talk in *The Merchant of Venice*.

Almost 30 years later, I began writing *Lost Daughter,* which not only engages with the themes of Canadian xenophobia and anti-Semitism in the summer of 1933, but also portrays the rich tradition of forgiveness in Jewish thought and culture. In the summer of 2008, on the 75th anniversary of the Christie Pits riot, the play was performed part of the Toronto Fringe Festival.

Ana's Shadow (2012)

The last play in the anthology, *Ana's Shadow*, is a contemporary drama that is a sequel to *Harriet's House*, a play written and performed in 2010. Both *Harriet's House* and *Ana's Shadow* examine the everyday experiences of transnational/transracial adoptive same-sex families. These are experiences that have not yet been widely documented or shared in educational research, nor widely discussed in teacher education classrooms. The research that has informed the plays comes from a set of interviews I conducted with people living in transnational/transracial adoptive same-sex families, as well as from a variety of personal narratives and documentary films about growing up and living in these families.

Harriet's House tells the story of Harriet's daughter Luisa, and her return to Bogotá to find her birth mother and connect with her Colombian linguistic and cultural heritage. *Ana's Shadow* picks up the story of Harriet's family three years later, and features the story of Luisa's sister, Ana, a singer-songwriter who has no interest in speaking Spanish with her sister or in returning to her birth country. Ana performs three original songs in *Ana's Shadow*: "Absent Impact", "Chanting" and "Heaven". All three songs were composed for the play by British singer/ songwriters Chantelle Pike and Hannah Dean of the singing duo, Eyes for Gertrude, and can be heard in a digital recording of a staged reading of *Ana's Shadow* that was produced by my theatre company, Gailey Road Productions, in 2013. The recording is available at www.gaileyroad.com

In choosing to research, write and teach about the lives of people living in transnational adoptive families, I hope not only to inform the work teachers do with these particular kinds of families, but also to inform the work teachers do with many other kinds of families, including: immigrant/newcomer families, mixed-race families, families learning English as a second or additional language, blended families, and families led by grandparents or other family members. In writing and teaching *two* plays, featuring the different experiences of two adopted daughters, I have tried to work against presenting a singular, dominant narrative of the experiences of transnationally adopted same-sex families.

In the last two years, I have begun to document the kinds of conversations and ideas that are provoked when my students read, perform and discuss the scripts. My documentation comes from notes on our class discussions, interviews with my students about the class discussions, and student journal entries and written assignments about their readings of the plays. To date, I have documented my work with the plays with six different classes. All together, 180 students have discussed and written about their work with the plays, and a small group of eight students (from the larger group of 180 students) has been interviewed about their experience of engaging with the play.

The most compelling finding of my research is that the work that the plays do is unpredictable. While my work with the plays sometimes provokes thoughtful reflection from my students about families that are different than their own, it does not always disrupt the prior, sometimes harmful, assumptions my students bring with them to teaching. Yet, within our class discussions, and in response to the journal entries and assignments my students write following our play readings and discussions, I am able to ask questions about the ways in which my students are engaging with the plays and the ways in which they are engaging in the project of learning about "Other people's families". Sometimes, I am able to raise a new idea, point out a generalization, and disrupt the compelling power of personal experience. In doing so, I am engaging in what educational researcher, Kevin Kumashiro describes as the "ongoing labour of stopping the repetition of harmful 'knowledges'" in my classroom (2000, p. 43). As well, having my students write journal entries and assignments about their work with the play immediately after our readings and conversations allows me some access to what was not said aloud in our class discussions. This, at times, can deepen my labour.

I hope that you enjoy reading all three plays and that you will want to use them in your own classrooms. If you do and want to share your experiences of working with the plays with me, I would love to hear from you.

All the best,
Tara Goldstein
Toronto, Ontario, Canada
September 2013

ACKNOWLEDGEMENTS

I would like to acknowledge the Social Sciences and Humanities Research Council of Canada (SSHRCC) for their funding of *Ana's Shadow*. I would also like to thank Irena Kohn for her expert editing and formatting of this book, Margot Huycke for her cover photo and Lisa Rupchand for the cover image.

NOTES

[1] See Saldaña (2005, pp. 10–14), for examples of work in many of these areas.

[2] *Hong Kong, Canada*, a play about immigration and multilingualism in a Canadian high school.

[3] The first critical ethnography focused on teaching English as a Second Language to women working in a bilingual Portuguese and English toy factory and was called *Two Languages at Work: Bilingual Life on the Production Floor* (Goldstein 1997). The second focused on teaching and learning in a bilingual Cantonese and English high school, and was called *Teaching and Learning in Multilingual School: Choices, Risks and Dilemmas* (Goldstein 2003) and includes the performed ethnography *Hong Kong, Canada*.

8

ZERO TOLERANCE

A Performance on the Pursuit of Safe Schools
Responding to the report *The Road to Health* (2008)

By The School Community Safety Advisory Panel that was commissioned by The Toronto District School Board

PRODUCTION HISTORY

Zero Tolerance was first performed as a staged reading at the Safe Schools Conference at the Ontario Institute for Studies in Education (OISE), University of Toronto on September 27, 2008. The reading was directed by Jocelyn Wickett and the staging that appears in the stage directions in this draft of the script was designed by Ms. Wickett for this inaugural performance. The PowerPoint slide show was designed by Dominique Rivère.

The performance was followed by a set of prepared responses from a panel that featured vice-principal and PhD candidate Dean Barnes from the Halton District School Board, one of OISE's partner school boards; Bev Caswell, an OISE teacher educator; Jeff Kugler, the executive director of OISE's Centre for Urban Schooling, and Charis Lo, a teacher candidate who had participated in the reading. A further two-hour discussion for audience members who wanted to discuss the report in some detail followed the performance. About 30 Bachelor of Education students, also known as teacher candidates, attended this discussion. Other teacher candidates at the Safe Schools Conference attended workshops on peace building, conflict resolution, and peer mediation that provided opportunities to discuss practical strategies for dealing with some of the issues raised by the performance. The OISE cast who performed the stage reading included:

Tara Goldstein   Tara Goldstein   Teacher Educator

Julian Falconer	Jeff Kugler	Exec Director, Centre for Urban Schooling
Peggy Edwards	Dominique Rivère	Research Officer, Centre for Urban Schooling
Linda McKinnon	Leslie Stewart Rose	Teacher Educator
Teacher 1	Pavlina Michailidis	Teacher candidate
Teacher 2	Issac Thomas	Teacher candidate
Teacher 3	Richard Ammah	Teacher candidate
Teacher 4	Charis Lo	Teacher candidate
Teacher 5	Keisha Morgan	Teacher candidate
Principal	Camille Dionne-West	Teacher candidate
Parent 1	Nicole West-Burns	Research Officer, Centre for Urban Schooling
Parent 2	James Berrigan	Secondary Teacher, Toronto District Board
Parent 3	Beverly Caswell	Teacher Educator
Media Reporter	Jason Martorino	Teacher candidate
HS Student 1	Kriss-Ann Cousley	Teacher candidate
HS Student 2	Nysha Johnston	Teacher candidate
HS Student 3	Marina Nikolovski	Teacher candidate

DEVELOPMENT HISTORY

The first draft of *Zero Tolerance* was completed in March 2008, shortly after the Toronto District School Board (TDSB) released *The Road to Health*, the report on school safety it commissioned from the School Community Safety Advisory Panel. TDSB high school teacher, Margot Huycke and a group of Bachelor of Education students enrolled in the Schooling and Sexualities course at the Ontario Institute of Studies Education (OISE), University of Toronto read the first draft of the script in March 2008. I revised the script and asked a second group of Bachelor of Education students and their teacher educators at OISE to do a reading of the second draft of the script. The next draft of the script was read with members of OISE's Centre of Urban Schooling and was also revised. The fourth draft of the script was rehearsed by a group of teacher educators and Bachelor of Education students who had volunteered to perform the script at the OISE Safe Schools Conference on September 27, 2008. After the fifth version of the script was performed at the conference, it was revised once more in response to the feedback I received from the staged reading.

A NOTE FROM THE PLAYWRIGHT

In May 2007, 15-year-old high school student, Jordan Manners was shot and killed in the hallway of his Toronto school. In June 2007, the Toronto District School Board commissioned an investigation into school safety, which resulted in a four-volume 595-page report, entitled *The Road to Health*. The report was released to the public on January 10, 2008, at a press conference convened by the Director of the Toronto District School Board.

One month later, in an attempt to provoke discussion about the investigative report among Bachelor of Education students and teacher educators in Toronto, I began to adapt *The Road to Health* into a performance script. The script, directed by MA student and theatre artist, Jocelyn Wickett, was performed in September 2008 for 500 teacher candidates at the Ontario Institute for Studies in Education (OISE)'s annual Safe Schools Conference.

When I began writing the script a month after The Road to Health had been released, the report had already begun to be discussed in the local media and in neighbourhood community forums. One of my first adaptation decisions was to include public responses to the report, as well as excerpts from the report itself in the performance script.

A second decision was imagining the audience that would be engaging with the performance script. OISE's annual Safe Schools Conference for initial teacher education students was an ideal venue for a performance of *The Road to Health*, so I decided to write the script for an audience of teacher candidates and their teacher educators, who were also my colleagues at OISE. These two early decisions provided me with several characters for the script: a media reporter and a group of five new teachers.

A third decision was to write myself into the script by giving myself the role of narrator. I made this decision because I felt it was important to remind the audience that the performance they were about to see was an interpretation of the report, only one of many that had been made by a number of educators, community leaders, government officials and the media since the report had been released. As educational researchers have been writing for decades now, writing up research data is an interpretative, subjective, value-laden project. I wanted my audience to remember that the performance they were seeing was constructed from my own ideas about the meaning the report had for my community at OISE.

My fourth decision was to project images on a screen behind the actors during the performance. The images I selected include photographs of the three members of the School Community Safety Advisory Panel who wrote the report: human rights lawyer, Julian Falconer; retired teacher, school administrator and superintendent of education, Linda MacKinnon, and community development worker and administrator, Peggy Edwards. The photographs are a visual reminder that the report itself, along with the recommendations it suggests for creating safer, healthier schools is a document that has been created by three particular individuals. It is also a reminder that the characters in the play are not the individuals portrayed on the screen. They have been created by a playwright who has taken excerpts from the report to suit the purposes of the story she wants to tell about what the shooting of Jordan Manners in the hallway of his school means for teachers.

CHARACTERS

TARA GOLDSTEIN: Playwright, teacher educator, white, middle-aged.

THE PANEL

JULIAN FALCONER: Human rights lawyer, biracial, middle-aged.
PEGGY EDWARDS: Social worker, black, middle-aged.
LINDA MCKINNON: Retired school teacher, white, middle-aged.

PRESERVICE TEACHERS   A racially, ethnically mixed group.

TEACHER 1
TEACHER 2
TEACHER 3
TEACHER 4
TEACHER 5

PRINCIPAL: White, middle-aged.

PARENTS

Parent 1:   Black, middle-aged, an activist.
Parent 2:   Black, middle-aged, an activist.
Parent 3:   White, middle-aged.

MEDIA REPORTER   White, any age.

HIGH SCHOOL STUDENTS   A racially, ethnically mixed group of young
                                    women.

STUDENT 1
STUDENT 2
STUDENT 3

SETTING

Toronto, Winter 2008

At rise: There is a screen upstage centre. On the screen, there is a slide with the following: *Zero Tolerance* by Tara Goldstein. A Research Performance on the Pursuit of Safe Schools based on the Report *The Road to Health* by the School Community Safety Advisory Panel (2008). The actors enter. Most of the actors form two groups centre stage. One group, sitting stage left, is made up of THE PANEL and the PRE-SERVICE TEACHERS. The second group, sitting stage right, is made up of THE PARENTS, THE PRINCIPAL and the HIGH SCHOOL STUDENTS. The PRE-SERVICE TEACHERS are wearing baseball caps with the logo "OISE/UT" on them. TARA GOLDSTEIN stands downstage left. The media reporter sits in the audience and during the performance moves around the stage taking photographs as first, THE PANEL, then, the

13

PARENTS and finally, the THE HIGH SCHOOL STUDENTS speak.

Scene 1 Zero Tolerance

TARA GOLDSTEIN
(To the audience) What do you think of when you hear the words "zero tolerance"? What comes to mind? When I asked a group of my students that question, this is what they said:

TEACHER 1
Bullying.

TEACHER 2
Fighting.

TEACHER 3
Weapons.

TEACHER 4
Suspension.

TEACHER 5
Expulsion.

TEACHER 2
No second chances.

TEACHER 4
Discipline.

TEACHER 5
Safety.

TARA GOLDSTEIN
(To audience, walking from downstage left, to downstage centre, to downstage right) Is that what you were thinking? Today, I am going

to tell you a story about zero tolerance for bad behaviour in schools. And how a zero tolerance approach to discipline has not protected students from violence in their schools. My story includes the story of a fifteen-year-old boy named Jordan Manners who was shot in his school during the school day in May 2007. My story also includes excerpts of a report on school safety commissioned by the Director of the Toronto District School Board after the shooting of Jordan Manners. As part of my story, you will hear how some parents, members of the community and the media reacted to the report. You will also hear how some teachers and principals responded. Finally, you'll hear what I think some of all this may mean for teachers and teacher educators at OISE/UT. *(Walking back to downstage left)* I will begin my story by introducing you to the three people who wrote the report *The Road to Health.*

Julian Falconer, human rights lawyer.
> *(FALCONER stands. On the screen is a photo of the real Julian Falconer.)*

Peggy Edwards, social worker.
> *(EDWARDS stands. On the screen is a photo of the real Peggy Edwards.)*

Linda McKinnon, retired school teacher.
> *(MCKINNON stands. On the screen is a photo of the real Linda McKinnon.)*

And now, I will introduce you to the people who have something to say about the report: a group of pre-service teachers from OISE.

(The TEACHERS stand.)

A principal at the Toronto District School Board.

(The PRINCIPAL stands.)

A group of parents.

(The PARENTS stand.)

A media reporter.

(The REPORTER stands up in the audience, waves and comes downstage left behind TARA GOLDSTEIN.)

15

And last, but certainly not least, a group of high school students at the Toronto District School Board.

(The STUDENTS stand.)

Now that you've met all the characters, let's get on with the story.

(Everyone but the panel sits. THE PANEL steps forward to downstage left.)

Scene 2 One Bullet Wounds Many

(On the screen, a picture of Jordan Manners, from the cover of the report Road to Health and the following appears: One Bullet Wounds Many.)

TARA GOLDSTEIN
One Bullet Wounds Many.

FALCONER
Jordan Manners was five days beyond his fifteenth birthday when he died on May 23, 2007, in the hallway of C.W. Jeffreys Secondary School as a result of a bullet wound to the chest.

EDWARDS
The students of C.W. Jeffreys honour his memory with a tribute that remains in the main hall of the school entitled "One Bullet Wounds Many".

MCKINNON
The death of Jordan Manners must serve as a wake-up call on the vulnerability of our youth to the dangers and tragedy of violence *inside* as well as outside our schools.

EDWARDS
We are the members of The School Community Safety Advisory Panel.

FALCONER

And after the shooting of Jordan Manners at C. W. Jeffreys, we were asked by the director of Toronto District School Board to investigate issues of violence and safety in its schools.

MCKINNON

The Board was interested in what was needed to maintain student order and discipline. It also wanted to know how to improve practices around school supervision, discipline and security so that its students can come to school and find a positive, safe and welcoming environment.

THE PANEL

There are 126 recommendations in our report.

FALCONER

The report includes discussions on guns and disciplinary measures in schools ...

EDWARDS

Missing supports for marginalized and complex needs students ...

MEDIA REPORTER

(Incredulous) Complex needs?!

MCKINNON

(Ignores Media Reporter) Violence against girls ...

EDWARDS

... and the breakdown in the relationship between students and teachers.

FALCONER

Our report was commissioned in response to the shooting of Jordan Manners. Let's begin with guns.

(THE PARENTS, THE TEACHERS and THE PRINCIPAL stand up and step forward to downstage left.)

Scene 3 Guns

(On the screen, the following appears: Guns)

TARA GOLDSTEIN

Guns.

FALCONER

Schools mirror the communities they serve. The ills that our communities face outside schools make their way into the schools.

PARENT 1

Schools mirror the *society* they serve. The ills that our *society* faces outside schools make their way into the schools.

MCKINNON

There is a community-wide crisis of confidence in the ability of schools to ensure violence-free and weapons-free environments.

MEDIA REPORTER

There aren't any guns in my kid's school.

THE PANEL

(Ignores Media Reporter) The Panel shares this concern.

FALCONER

There are guns in select schools across Toronto in serious numbers.

EDWARDS

The question you want to ask, of course, is "Who's carrying the guns?" "Who represents the greatest safety concern?"

MCKINNON

Our answer is this: Students who are disengaged with school. Students who aren't succeeding academically.

FALCONER

And who are *they*?

EDWARDS

Students from our marginalized communities. In the report, we call them "marginalized youth".

MCKINNON

And students with complex socio-psychological health needs. In the report, we call them "complex-needs youth".

TEACHER 3

Don't all youth have "complex needs?"

FALCONER

We deliberately use the terms marginalized youth and complex-needs youth instead of "high-risk" youth or youth "at risk".

TEACHER 3

Oh. Why?

FALCONER

High-risk or at risk means the students are about to step in "do-do". Reality tells us that the students we're talking about are beyond the stage of risk. They've already stepped in "do-do". Some of them are knee-high in it.

TEACHER 4

So we're talking about students who are in trouble.

EDWARDS

When we talk about "marginalized youth" in the report, we do so to highlight the class, racial and achievement gaps these youth face.

MCKINNON

And when we talk about "complex-needs youth" we are talking about a larger class of youth, who experience disengagement and alienation due to other unique challenges that marginalized youth don't typically face.

TEACHER 4

Students who are behavioural. In special education.

FALCONER

So, how have schools dealt with youth who are disengaged?

THE PANEL

With zero tolerance.

EDWARDS

In 2002, The Tory Government amended the *Safe Schools Act.* Suspensions and expulsion were made mandatory for many forms of student misconduct.

MCKINNON

This ushered in an era of "zero tolerance".

(On the screen, the following list of grounds for suspension appears in green font: (1) threatening to inflict serious bodily harm on another person; possessing alcohol or illegal drugs; (2) being under the influence of alcohol; swearing at a teacher or another person in a position of authority; (3) vandalism that causes extensive damage to school property or to another person's property at school; (4) engaging in an activity that is not permitted under the school board's code of conduct.)

FALCONER

Students were to be suspended for (1) threatening to inflict serious bodily harm on another person; possessing alcohol or illegal drugs; (2) being under the influence of alcohol; swearing at a teacher or another person in a position of authority; (3) vandalism that causes extensive damage to school property or to another person's property at school or (4) engaging in an activity that is not permitted under the school board's code of conduct.

(On the screen, the following list of grounds for expulsion appears in red font: (1) possessing a weapon, including a knife or a gun; (2) using a weapon to cause, or threaten to cause, bodily harm to another person; physical assault that causes bodily harm requiring medical treatment; (3) sexual assault; trafficking in weapons or illegal drugs; robbery; giving alcohol to a minor; (4) engaging in an activity that is not permitted under the school board's code of conduct.)

EDWARDS
And they were to be expelled for (1) possessing a weapon, including a knife or a gun; (2) using a weapon to cause, or threaten to cause, bodily harm to another person; physical assault that causes bodily harm requiring medical treatment; (3) sexual assault; trafficking in weapons or illegal drugs; robbery; giving alcohol to a minor or (4) engaging in an activity that is not permitted under the school board's code of conduct.

TEACHER 4
As they should be.

FALCONER
But there was a problem in implementation.

MCKINNON
Youth were suspended and expelled in droves.

PARENT 1
(Calls out) Forty-thousand learners were denied an education.[1]

FALCONER
That was one of the parents we heard from after the report came out.

21

MCKINNON
Before the *Safe Schools Act* amendments, principals were only allowed to suspend students, not expel them. Only the school board could expel students.

EDWARDS
And before the *Safe Schools Act* amendments, the principal and the school boards were given discretion to determine whether or not suspension or expulsion was actually necessary. Students could only be expelled if their conduct was so "refractory" that their presence was "injurious to other pupils or persons".

TEACHER 3
What does "refractory" mean?

TEACHER 4
Disobedient.

TEACHER 3
Right.

MCKINNON
The *Safe Schools Act* amendments changed the way discipline was enforced in Ontario schools.

FALCONER
People told us that the amendments created a zero tolerance regime in Ontario. Despite the fact that there were provisions for mitigating factors.

(On the screen, the following list of mitigating factors appears in blue font: (1) a student did not have the ability to control his or her behaviour; (2) a student did not have the ability to understand the foreseeable consequences of his or her behaviour and (3) a student's continuing presence in the school did not create an unacceptable risk to the safety of any person.)

EDWARDS

Suspension or expulsion was *not* mandatory if (1) a student did not have the ability to control his or her behaviour,

MCKINNON

(2) a student did not have the ability to understand the foreseeable consequences of his or her behaviour,

FALCONER

Or (3) a student's continuing presence in the school did not create an unacceptable risk to the safety of any person.

EDWARDS

People told us that students were suspended and expelled without any consideration of these mitigating factors.

TEACHER 3

No consideration of mitigating factors?

EDWARDS

And people told us that suspensions and expulsions were applied in a discriminatory manner. Against students of colour and students with disabilities.

MCKINNON

After reviewing suspension and expulsion data collected from the Board …

THE PANEL

We agree.

MEDIA REPORTER

Aren't you glossing over the fact that schools in black areas are more dangerous than schools in other areas? To be politically correct?

PRINCIPAL

Not everyone suspended and expelled students without looking at mitigating factors. The policy was there, but some principals *did* look at mitigating factors.

TARA GOLDSTEIN

That was one of the school principals *I* talked to after the report came out.

FALCONER

We call this new culture of suspension and expulsion the "Safe Schools Culture", and we believe that it has hurt Toronto's

THE PANEL

Most disenfranchised.

PARENT 2

The Conservative government misdiagnosed the situation.

FALCONER

That is another parent we heard from after the report came out.

PARENT 2

Schools are unsafe because a number of our communities are in crisis. We need to address the issues that put our communities in crisis. At the same time that it passed the *Safe Schools Act*, the Conservative government also drastically cut the education budget. Out went the youth workers. In came the police.

PARENT 1

(Calls out) Forty-thousand learners were denied an education.

PARENT 2

As a society, we have failed our children.

EDWARDS
The Safe Schools Culture preaches a theory that complex-needs youth should be "treated the same" as all other youth.

MEDIA REPORTER
But these kids are violent.

MCKINNON
Students are then pushed out of the schools and onto the streets.

EDWARDS
Without supports.

FALCONER
And did the Safe School Culture succeed in making schools violence-free and weapons-free?

THE PANEL
No.

EDWARDS
The death of Jordan Manners speaks for itself.

> *(Everyone returns to their seats and sits down except THE STUDENTS, who remain standing and THE TEACHERS, who remain standing and walk to upstage centre.)*

> *(On the screen, a picture of Jordan Manners from the cover of the report The Road to Health and the following appears: One Bullet Wounds Many.)*

TEACHER 1
On May 23, 2007, Jordan Manners was scheduled to attend four classes.

TEACHER 2
Period One – Applied Geography.

TEACHER 3
Period Two – Learning Strategies.

TEACHER 4
Period Four – Visual Arts.

TEACHER 5
Period Five – Introduction to Information Technology in Business.

TEACHER 1
Period three is lunch.

TEACHER 2
The attendance counselor at C.W Jeffreys says she met with Jordan Manners at approximately 1:10 pm to give him an admit slip to class and to update his file with contact numbers for his family.

TEACHER 3
This conversation shows that Jordan Manners was in the school building and on his way– late – to his period four class. Visual Arts.

TEACHER 1
I teach Visual Arts. Jordan Manners could have been my student.

TEACHER 4
The admit slip provided by the attendance counselor was required for him to gain admission to his period four class. His teacher marked him as present.

TEACHER 1
Visual Arts was Jordan Manners' last class.

TEACHER 5
Ordinarily, Jordan would have been dismissed from class at 1:50, and would have had five minutes to get to his period five class at 1:55.

TEACHER 2
Period five was Introduction to Information and Technology in Business and the classroom, Room 107, is located on the main floor of the school, but in a wing that is below ground level.

TEACHER 3
What happened next isn't clear.

TEACHER 4
One student in the period five class said that Jordan was initially present, but that he asked to be excused to use the washroom.

TEACHER 5
But Jordan was recorded as being absent from the period five class.

TEACHER 2
The same student also said that Jordan didn't return to class, and that the next time he saw him, he was lying in the hallway, one level up, on the main floor.

TEACHER 3
The Panel is not able to trace Jordan Manners' precise movements from the time he left his period five class to the time that he was found in "medical distress" by a teacher at approximately 2:15 or 2:20.

TEACHER 4
The teacher was returning to his own class in Room 106, after delivering his attendance sheet to the main office.

TEACHER 1
It could have been me.

TEACHER 5
Jordan Manners was lying on his stomach.

TEACHER 2

The teacher saw three girls in the immediate vicinity. His first impression was that they were wrestling with an unknown boy on the floor.

TEACHER 3

But as he got closer, he saw that it was Jordan Manners and he was moving in a jerky convulsive way.

TEACHER 4

The teacher sensed that the three girls didn't understand what was happening.

TEACHER 5

Then he realized the boy was in distress, and within seconds, recognized him as Jordan Manners.

TEACHER 2

He asked the girls what happened, but they seemed confused and didn't respond.

TEACHER 3

The teacher attempted to get a response from Jordan, but was unsuccessful.

TEACHER 4

The teacher's classroom was closer than the office, so he went back to his room to contact the main office by intercom.

TEACHER 5

He tried twice to get a response from the main office, but was unsuccessful.

TEACHER 2

Can you imagine how he felt?

TEACHER 1

It could have been me.

TEACHER 3

The teacher went back into the hallway and saw one of the hall monitors.

TEACHER 4

He told the hall monitor what had happened and the hall monitor contacted the office on his handheld radio.

TEACHER 5

One of the secretaries received the radio call.

TEACHER 2

She immediately told another secretary to call 911 and then tried to retrieve the first aid kit.

TEACHER 3

She couldn't get it out of the drawer. Why couldn't she get it out of the drawer?

TEACHER 4

So she left it there, and ran towards the location where Jordan Manners was lying.

TEACHER 5

When she got there, she checked for a pulse.

TEACHER 2

She noted that he was still breathing and seemed to be gasping for breath.

TEACHER 3

She thought that he was looking at her and was still conscious.

TEACHER 4

But he couldn't speak.

TEACHER 5

Seconds later, the secretary was joined by one of the special needs assistants and the head secretary.

TEACHER 2

The head secretary had retrieved the first aid kit.

TEACHER 3

The three staff members turned Jordan Manners on his side.

TEACHER 4

And then on his back.

TEACHER 5

But his breathing became more difficult when he was on his back, so they turned him back onto his side.

TEACHER 2

At this time, no one saw any trauma.

TEACHER 3

No one saw any blood.

TEACHER 4

He was still having trouble breathing so they tried to take off his jacket and shirt with some scissors from the first aid kit.

TEACHER 5

The hall monitor noticed a hole in Jordan's jacket as it was being removed, but didn't realize that he had been shot.

TEACHER 2

After his shirt was removed, the secretary noticed a "dot" in the middle of Jordan's chest.

TEACHER 3

But it didn't appear to be a recent injury.

TEACHER 4

Jordan was still breathing at this stage. His eyes were blinking and he appeared to be attempting to lift his arm.

TEACHER 5

It was about five minutes after the radio call to the office.

TEACHER 2

The staff tried to keep him comfortable.

TEACHER 3

They fanned his face with a sheet of cardboard.

TEACHER 4

And put an icepack behind his neck.

TEACHER 1

It could have been me.

TEACHER 5

Before the ambulance arrived, the secretary saw another student from C.W. Jeffreys in the hallway adjacent to Jordan Manners.

TEACHER 2

He was speaking on a cell phone.

TEACHER 3

The secretary thought he was trying to contact Jordan Manners' family.

TEACHER 4

Later, this student would be one of the youths charged in relation to Jordan Manners' death.

TEACHER 5

The ambulance arrived about ten minutes after 911 was called.

HIGH SCHOOL STUDENT 1

(Outraged) Why did it take ten minutes for the ambulance to arrive?

TARA GOLDSTEIN

That was one of the students at C.W. Jeffreys.

TEACHER 2

Two EMS personnel took care of Jordan.

TEACHER 3

The secretary alerted them to the mark on his chest.

TEACHER 4

She thought a firecracker might have caused it.

TEACHER 5

There had been several serious incidents the day before, which was the day after Victoria Day, with firecrackers being set off in the hallways.

TEACHER 2

But one of the EMS personnel said he thought the mark was a gunshot wound.

TEACHER 3

They worked on Jordan for about ten to fifteen minutes at the school.

TEACHER 4

They started CPR.

TEACHER 5

When more EMS personnel arrived, they took Jordan out of the school on an ambulance gurney.

HIGH SCHOOL STUDENT 1

Why did they have to wait?

TEACHER 2

The police arrived just before the ambulance left.

TEACHER 3

The police officers told the staff to close off the hallway in which Jordan had been located.

TEACHER 4

And then the school went into lockdown.

TEACHER 5

Until about 6:00 pm.

HIGH SCHOOL STUDENT 1

No one left their classroom.

TEACHER 2

The secretary went back to the main office.

TEACHER 3

And she saw the student who had been on the cell phone in a conference room in the main office area.

TEACHER 4

She said he was in a state of panic.

TEACHER 5

Making numerous calls on his cell.

TEACHER 2
At one stage, she saw him crying.

TEACHER 3
Four days later, on May 28, 2007, that student, along with another 17-year old youth, was arrested in connection with Jordan Manners' death.

(Pause. THE PANEL stands up and walks downstage right. THE PARENTS and THE PRINCIPAL stand up and walk downstage left.)

FALCONER
While you will insist, of course, that "one is too many", the question you also want to ask is: "But how often does such a thing happen? How prevalent is gun-related violence in our schools?"

EDWARDS
There are guns in select schools across Toronto in serious numbers.

TEACHER 4
How do you know this?

MCKINNON
We know this from the information we collected from the Board's Weekly Incident Report and Crisis Reports. The Incident and Crisis Reports tell us that gun violence is a problem at a number of schools *across* the Board. C.W Jeffreys and its neighbour, Westview Centennial Secondary School, the two schools that we studied in depth, should not be singled out. The gun problem is not limited to one community.

PARENT 2
A number of communities are in crisis.

PARENT 3
Not my community. There are no guns in my kid's school.

FALCONER
(Ignores Parent 3) So what do we do about the guns? Metal detectors, a tempting response to guns, are not going to transform unsafe schools into safe schools.

EDWARDS
It's a very complex problem. A multi-faceted approach is needed.

MCKINNON
We believe that school safety depends on school health.

THE PANEL
If schools are healthy then schools will be safe.

EDWARDS
Working with youth who are carrying the guns is the way forward.

MEDIA REPORTER
Locking them up in jail is the way forward.

MCKINNON
(Ignores Media Reporter) A new vision, a new approach is needed. It should include discipline, such as suspension and expulsion, but …

EDWARDS
… It should also be capable of operating beyond straight enforcement.

FALCONER
The fundamental challenge for schools is to identify and implement key strategies to re-engage youth.

EDWARDS
This means understanding students' unique circumstances.

PARENT 2
A number of our communities are in crisis.

PARENT 3

Not my community. There are no guns in my kid's school.

MCKINNON

(Ignores Parent 3) Youth who come to school unable to learn because of their challenging lives outside of school have needs that must be addressed through social services and inclusive curriculum aimed at their realities.

THE PANEL

This isn't just a school problem.

EDWARDS

We must deal with matters beyond academics and school discipline.

FALCONER

And this requires a coordinated effort by all relevant arms of government and community agencies.

MCKINNON

Many of our 126 recommendations outline what needs to happen to make this kind of coordinated effort a reality.

EDWARDS

But there are no "quick fix" solutions.

MCKINNON

Years of neglect of marginalized communities have brought us to where we are today. Reversing the trends will not be accomplished overnight. But one thing is clear.

THE PANEL

Marginalized youth cannot be punished into being engaged.

FALCONER

Mass suspensions and conventional discipline for youth won't work.

EDWARDS

What will work are programs and initiatives that create prospects for youth who are currently on the outside looking in.

> (On the screen, the following appears: "It's easier to get a gun than to get a job".)

MCKINNON

Youth tell us, "It's easier to get a gun than to get a job".

> (On the screen, the following appears: "Let's make it easier to get the job".)

FALCONER

"Let's make it easier to get the job."

THE PANEL

Dismantling the Safe Schools Culture is imperative.

EDWARDS

But this is difficult to do.

MCKINNON

The legacy of zero tolerance policies continues to hang over the Board's Safe Schools Department. The Department is now called the Safe and Caring Schools Department, but the vestiges of its Safe Schools Culture are still present.

FALCONER

So, what can be done? The Panel recommends a new approach that infuses equity into youth management, through a new Department called the "Well-Being and Equity Department."

EDWARDS

This will ensure that that there will be no discipline without equity.

PARENT 3

Or no discipline at all.

MCKINNON

(Ignores Parent 3) The job of the Well-Being and Equity Department will be to work to end the Safe Schools Culture at the Board.

PARENT 1

Forty-thousand learners were denied an education.

(Pause.)

TARA GOLDSTEIN

Now let's talk about the girls.

(Everyone stays standing.)

Scene 4 Violence Against Girls

(On the screen, the following appears: Violence Against Girls.)

TARA GOLDSTEIN

Violence against girls.

FALCONER

Soon after the Panel began its work, we uncovered an undisclosed sexual assault at C.W. Jeffreys.

TARA GOLDSTEIN

The specifics of the alleged assault are still under investigation, so the story that the Panel tells here should not be understood as a closed case.

EDWARDS

In 2006, before the shooting of Jordan Manners, several students reported the sexual assault of a young, female student of colour in the school.

HIGH SCHOOL STUDENT 2

We came forward because the boys were picking on girls who weren't popular and had no friends.

MCKINNON

The current policy requires that sexual assaults be reported to police and that principals and vice-principals take direction from police concerning the informing of parents.

EDWARDS

But because of the young woman's ethnic and religious background, the principal and vice-principals did not notify the police or the student's parents about the incident. They were worried that she'd be further abused by her parents if they found out.

FALCONER

As news about the incident began to circulate in the school, the student became the subject of intense sexual harassment and ridicule by other students. Although the principal and vice-principal took steps to curb this abusive behaviour, the bullying continued.

HIGH SCHOOL STUDENT 3

The teachers and principals couldn't protect her.

MCKINNON

Eventually, at her own request, the young woman transferred to another school.

TEACHER 1

This happens more frequently than I thought.

EDWARDS

Because the sexual assault was not reported to the police or to parents, no steps were taken to remove the alleged perpetrators from the school.

HIGH SCHOOL STUDENT 2
Nothing was done until these people heard about it and told someone.

FALCONER
After finding out about the incident, the Director of the Board reported it to the police and an investigation was initiated. Then, the Director of the Board requested that the Panel add to its more general investigation on school violence and school safety, a particular examination of violence against girls at school.

MCKINNON
There are several very troubling dimensions to the sexual assault incident at C.W. Jeffreys.

FALCONER
First, a female student was victimized at school, not only by other students, but also by the delayed and inadequate response from the school system that was supposed to protect her.

HIGH SCHOOL GIRL 3
The teachers and principals couldn't protect her.

EDWARDS
Second, no steps were taken to deal with the male students who were allegedly involved, so other female students may have been placed at risk.

MCKINNON
Third, stereotypes about ethnicity and religion appear to have played a role in the principals' decision to not follow the Board's sexual assault policy.

PRINCIPAL
But what do you do if your student *tells* you she'll be further abused if her parents find out?

FALCONER

While, thankfully, shootings in and around Toronto schools are still a relatively rare occurrence, the same cannot be said about sexual harassment and sexual assault. According to our survey of students at C.W. Jeffreys and Westview, violence against girls is pervasive.

EDWARDS

Twenty-nine female students, seven percent of all the female respondents, all answered yes to the following question: "In the past two years, have you been sexually assaulted at school? Has someone ever forced you to have sex at school against your will?"

TEACHER 1

Twenty-nine young women answered yes.

MCKINNON

And twenty-one percent reported that they knew of at least one student who was sexually assaulted at school over the past two years.

TEACHER 1

Twenty-one percent. One in five.

TEACHER 4

But those numbers only refer to the students in those two schools.

TEACHER 5

They're not as high in other schools.

THE PANEL

(Ignores TEACHERS 4 AND 5) The seriousness of this problem requires immediate attention.

EDWARDS

Current anti-bullying programs are not effective in preventing violence against girls.

FALCONER

They are often gender-neutral and treat children and youth as a uniform group.

EDWARDS

We need to examine the roots of violence against girls.

MCKINNON

To talk about healthy relationships and equality among marginalized groups.

FALCONER

And counsel the boys who engage in sexual misconduct.

EDWARDS

The Board also needs to develop a new comprehensive Sexual Assault and Gender-Based Violence policy.

TEACHER 1

The new policy also needs to fight homophobia as well as sexual harassment and sexual assault.

TEACHER 2

There are 40 students who transferred out of their home schools to the Triangle Program this year because of homophobic bullying and harassment. Forty.

TEACHER 1

Forty students, all completing high school in a church basement, with only two teachers to teach the entire curriculum in four different grades: 9, 10, 11 and 12. But the students are happy to be there, because they finally feel safe.

TEACHER 2

Well, safer, anyway.

MCKINNON
(Nods at the students, but moves on) Current policy requires sexual assaults to be reported to police and that principals and vice-principals take direction from police concerning the informing of parents.

EDWARDS
But sexual assault experts agree that this policy of automatic reporting prevents some girls from coming forward.

FALCONER
For that reason, girls 16 years or older should be allowed to determine whether to report an incident to police or parents.

PRINCIPAL
What do you do if your student *tells* you that she'll be further abused if her parents find out?

FALCONER
And principals and vice-principals should consult with girls younger than 16 to assess whether there is a pressing reason for them not to report an incident to police or parents.

TEACHER 4
What's a pressing reason?

PARENT 2
I think parents have the right to know if their daughters have been assaulted.

PARENT 3
There are some decisions that shouldn't be made by young girls. Not telling a parent about a sexual assault is one of them. Girls need their parents' support.

EDWARDS

Female students must feel that their safety is a priority. They must feel that their concerns are being heard, and that a response will be given even if the incident is not reported. At present, this not the case.

HIGH SCHOOL STUDENT 3

The teachers and principals couldn't protect her.

EDWARDS

Principal discretion around reporting a sexual assault to police or parents should not result in nothing being done. Perpetrators of sexual violence must be dealt with. The levels of violence against girls in Toronto schools are unacceptable.

TEACHER 3

This happens more frequently than I thought.

THE PANEL

Immediate action is required.

TEACHER 2

But what kind of action can we take?

HIGH SCHOOL STUDENT 1

How could she have been protected?

MCKINNON

We need to break the silence around violence against girls in school. We need to break the silence around all forms of violence in school.

FALCONER

We need new security measures, improved accountability of trustees, and, perhaps, most important of all, we need a renewed relationship between teachers and students. A relationship that can create a positive bond between them.

(Everyone remains standing. THE STUDENTS and THE TEACHERS move to stand together downstage centre, while THE PANEL stands downstage right.)

Scene 5 Renewed Relationships Between Teachers and Students

(On the screen, the following appears: Renewed relationships between teachers and students.)

TARA GOLDSTEIN

Renewed relationships between teachers and students.

EDWARDS

Both teachers and students surveyed at C.W. Jeffreys and Westview reported that there are many students at their schools who do not respect their teachers.

MCKINNON

Further data from consultations with various teachers' unions, parents' associations and student focus groups tell us that this breakdown in the student-teacher relationship is a growing trend, not only at Jeffreys and Westview, but in all schools across the Board.

FALCONER

So what is causing the breakdown? Why are students not respecting their teachers?

EDWARDS

There are many factors. Here are six of them.

MCKINNON

Factor number one: Racism, both real and perceived, by members of the school community. Some students told us that they are singled out for unmerited discipline based on their race. It's not surprising, then, that students of colour feel isolated from their school.

FALCONER

Factor number two: Lack of support for complex-needs youth.

EDWARDS

Factor number three: Increase in delinquent behaviour by youth.

MCKINNON

Factor number four: Lack of teacher classroom management training. Teachers working in schools that serve marginalized and complex-needs youth need to be trained in effective practices that work in these particular kinds of schools.

TEACHER 2

Classroom management? Or community building? Teachers need to be trained in community building.

FALCONER

(Ignores Teacher 2) Factor number five: Lack of engagement of marginalized and complex-needs youth. The present pedagogy teachers are using in schools is not working for these students. Listen to what one of the high school students we interviewed has to say:

HIGH SCHOOL STUDENT 1

If you are gonna be teaching here and then 50 percent or 60 percent of your students actually fail or drop out or feel that there is no hope, no one cares about them, maybe there is something you are doing wrong. The approach that has been taken here is not working for a lot of kids, a lot of kids are still feeling left out.

EDWARDS

Factor number six: Lack of engagement by some teachers at schools serving marginalized and complex needs youth. Listen to what another student we interviewed had to say:

HIGH SCHOOL STUDENT 3

Get teachers who actually want to teach here. Do not just put someone here because they are a teacher and they have to be here. Show it, show that you actually care. I always say, your mouth is made to say anything, your action is what shows it.

THE PANEL
We agree.

FALCONER
Teachers who do not want to teach at schools serving marginalized and complex needs communities should be able to transfer out of the school without any negative consequences.

MCKINNON
Teaching students from marginalized and complex needs communities is not an easy task. Teachers must understand and be alive to the unique social and economic conditions affecting students from these communities.

PARENT 1
It's not only about the "conditions" our kids live in. It's not only about their "complex needs". It's about the skills and talents and resilience our kids bring to schools that teachers don't recognize. Don't take the time to learn about.

EDWARDS
Handling the pressures that are associated with these conditions can cause teachers a great deal of stress. Teachers who may request a transfer from schools in marginalized and complex needs communities are not bad teachers. They just need a respite from the stresses of the job.

FALCONER
But teachers cannot be given the sole responsibility for addressing all these students' needs. As we said earlier, extra staff supports are needed. Youth workers, social workers, counselors.

MCKINNON
Addressing the issues of each of these six factors is important for improving and renewing relationships between teachers and students.

THE PANEL

Renewing relationships is essential.

(TARA GOLDSTEIN walks to downstage centre. On the screen, a picture of Jordan Manners from the cover of the report The Road to Health and the following appears: One Bullet Wounds Many.)

TARA GOLDSTEIN

And on that note of the need for renewal, my story about zero tolerance and creating safe schools comes to an end. Teachers in Ontario have inherited the consequences of zero tolerance policies and practices and an ongoing legacy of racism, sexism, homophobia, classism and other forms of discrimination in schooling. And even though creating safe schools means dealing with matters "beyond academics", there is plenty teachers can do to create healthier learning environments. What are we doing at OISE to help teachers productively respond to discrimination in schools? Are we talking about how to respond to violence against girls? To homophobic bullying? Are teachers learning how to build community in their classrooms? To manage and resolve conflict through communication, as well as discipline? Are they learning to develop curriculum that is relevant to their students' lives? What else can teachers be doing? How should they be doing it? How can we do our part at OISE to work against another shooting at a Toronto school? *(Pause.)* Like Bendale.

TEACHERS

How can we do our part?

PRINCIPAL

(Joins the STUDENTS and TEACHERS) How can we do our part?

PARENTS

(Join the STUDENTS and TEACHERS) How can we do our part?

THE MEDIA REPORTER

(Joins the STUDENTS and TEACHERS) How can we do our part?

ALL

How can we do our part?
End of play

This performance entitled *Zero Tolerance* includes excerpts from and responses to *The Road to Health,* a report on school safety commissioned by the Toronto District School Board in early June 2007. The goal of the report was to analyze the events leading up to the tragic death of student Jordan Manners at C.W. Jefferys CI in May 2007, and to provide a set of recommendations for how to work towards safer schools. The report can be viewed and downloaded from the Toronto District Board's website:

www.tdsb.on.ca

What has happened at the Toronto District School Board since the release of the report
Updated: October 7, 2011

Since its release of the report to the pubic on January 10, 2008, the Toronto District School Board has begun to respond to some of the 126 recommendations listed in the report.

2008
In their staff newsletter dated February 2008, the Board listed a number of steps that had already been taken in response to the report. The Board had (1) launched a Student Safety Line so that students could have an anonymous way to report personal and school-related safety concerns; (2) established a Leadership Action Team to co-ordinate the overall strategy for addressing the Panel's report and (3) begun a review of all policies and procedures related to sexual and gender-based violence.

Between February and June 2008, the Board planned to establish (4) new Safe and Caring Schools Alternative Programs for expelled students; (5) evaluate key recommendations affecting staffing for

2008-09; (6) present a progress report about the work of the Leadership Action Team, and (7) complete their review of policies and procedures related to sexual and gender-based violence.

The Leadership Action Team released its report in May 2008 and the Safe Schools Action Team released its report in December 2008.

2009

Working with the findings of all three reports, in October 2009 the Board created a Gender-Based Violence Prevention team whose mandate is to develop and implement board-wide prevention programs focused on student awareness and 'healthy relationship education' and to coordinate existing resources to supports through board-wide prevention strategy to be integrated into all subject areas.

2010

In the spring of 2010, the Toronto District School Board implemented a new Gender-Based Violence Policy and new procedures for responding to sexual misconduct by students. For copies of the policy and procedures see:

http://www.tdsb.on.ca/wwwdocuments/programs/gender_based_ violence_prevention_gbvp_/docs/GBVP%20policy.pdf

http://www.tdsb.on.ca/wwwdocuments/programs/gender_based_ violence_prevention_gbvp_/docs/PR608%20Sexual%20Misconduct. pdf

In the fall of 2010, the (first) Africentric Alternative School at the Toronto District School Board opened under the leadership of Principal Thando Hyman. The school accepts students from JK to Grade 5 and has three key outcomes for its students: high academic achievement, high self-pride, and a high motivation to succeed. A unique feature of the school is its integration of the diverse perspectives, experiences and histories of people of African descent into the provincially mandated curriculum. The program also features a Parenting and Family Literacy Centre for pre-school children.

What has happened at C.W. Jeffreys since the release of the report

2010

In the three years since Jordan Manners' death, new co-curricular activities such as football, cheerleading, leadership camps, a boys' leadership group and a girls' leadership group were established at C. W. Jeffreys. The school also has a School Resource Officer who coaches volleyball, provides curriculum support in the school's law classes and helps build student awareness around issues of gangs and bullying. And in the fall of 2010, the school offered its first parent workshop to parents of students at C.W. Jeffreys.

ACKNOWLEDGEMENTS

I want to thank and acknowledge the OISE faculty, students and researchers who performed the staged reading of *Zero Tolerance* at the Safe Schools Conference. I also want to thanks and acknowledge Jocelyn Wickett who directed the reading, and Dominique Rivère who provided additional research support for the project and who designed the PowerPoint slide show we used in the staged reading. Finally, thanks go to OISE Professor Kathy Bickmore and PhD student James Berrigan for their interest in this project and their organizational support.

NOTES

[1] The figure of 40,000 students, used to refer to the number of students suspended and expelled during the zero tolerance era, was cited at a community forum entitled: A Forum on School Safety and Equity: Community Responses to the Falconer Report. The forum was held on March 4, 2008 and was sponsored by the Black Action Defense Committee, The Miss G Project, MPP Rosario Marchese, Toronto District School Board (TDSB) School Trustee Chris Bolton, Toronto Coalition for Equity in Education and the Urban Alliance on Race Relations. It was not clear if the panel speaker, Yolisa Dalemba from the parent group Reclaiming our Children, was referring to the number of suspended and expelled students at the TDSB, or in the province of Ontario. However, further consultation with teacher educator and TDSB vice-principal, Belinda Longe (personal communication), revealed that depending on how one added up the numbers, it was possible that the figure of 40,000 students was referring to the number of suspended and expelled students at the Toronto District School Board over the course of the many years during which the zero tolerance policy was in place. A similar figure was recently used in an article on "turning gang members into community activists" in *Now Magazine*. The article reports that there were 17,371 suspensions across the TDSB in 2001-2002 and 24,238 a year later in 2001-2002 (*Now Magazine* July 17-23, 2008).

LOST DAUGHTER

PRODUCTION HISTORY

Lost Daughter was first professionally produced by Gailey Road Productions on July 3, 2008, at the Al Green Theatre as part of the 2008 Toronto Fringe Festival, with the following cast:

Esther	NADINE RABINOVITCH
Jessica	SOCHI FRIED
Larry	JOSHUA LEWIS
Pat	ELICIA CRONIN
Bradley	TYLER SEGUIN
Shimon	PAUL SOREN
Director:	JOCELYN WICKETT
Production Design:	ELIZABETH NUTTING
Publicity Director:	IRENA KOHN
Publicity Assistant:	YUVRAJ JOSHI
Stage Manager:	GILLIAN LEWIS

DEVELOPMENT HISTORY

Early drafts of *Lost Daughter* were read and critiqued by dramaturges Eric Schmiedl from Spalding University in the spring of 2005; by Kent Stetson from the PEI Conservatory in the summer of 2005, by Emma Tibold from Playwrights' Workshop Montreal in the fall of 2005; and by Jennifer Caparu from Factory Theatre in the winter of 2006.

A rehearsed reading of *Lost Daughter* was performed at the Sarasota Jewish Theater's Playreading Series at The Flanzer Jewish Community Centre in Sarasota, Florida on November 4 and 5, 2006. The play reading was directed by Sharon Lesley, and the cast was as follows:

Esther	CAROLYN MEEKER
Jessica	KATHRYN OHRENSTEIN
Larry	DONALD DUPRESS
Pat	ERIN RACHAEL SCHWARTZ
Bradley	ANDRZEJ MROTEK
Shimon	JEFF GOLDMAN

As the winner of the 2005 Canadian Jewish Playwriting Contest, *Lost Daughter* was given a rehearsed reading at the Miles Nadal Jewish Community Centre's Between Stages Playwright's Reading Series in Toronto, on April 29, 2007. The play reading was directed by Anthony Furey. The cast was as follows:

Esther	CAROLINE AZAR
Jessica	CHALA HUNTER
Larry	DANIEL KARASIK
Pat	TOVA SMITH
Bradley	NICHOLAS CARELLA
Shimon	WILLIAM WEBSTER

Finally, *Lost Daughter* was performed by community theatre troupe ACT Ottawa, in Ottawa, Kansas on August 2007. The production was directed by Jeanne Haggard. The cast was as follows:

Esther	KIM CONARD
Jessica	JO YOHE
Larry	TYLER BRYANT
Pat	MEGAN LOWRY
Bradley	DAKOTA YOHE
Shimon	TIM CONARD
Assistant Director	ANGIE PARKER

A NOTE FROM THE PLAYWRIGHT

Lost Daughter is an historical drama inspired by William Shakespeare's *The Merchant of Venice*. It is set in the Canadian city of Toronto in the summer of 1933, a summer of intense heat and widespread unemployment. It was a summer when Gentile youth wore swastika badges to keep the city's Jews out of public parks and away from beaches.

I had wanted to write this play ever since I was a high school student in another Canadian city, the city of Montreal. *The Merchant of Venice* was required reading in our grade nine English class, and I was chosen to read aloud the part of Shylock. The year was 1971, and the majority of the students in the English class, like me, were of Jewish background. Yet the binary of Christian forgiveness (most explicitly expressed in Portia's "quality of mercy" speech) and Jewish revenge (most explicitly symbolized by Shylock's desire for a pound of flesh) in the play was never discussed. At the end of our play reading, the Jewish students in the class were left with the uncomfortable suggestion that Christians were merciful, and Jews, who were vengeful, needed to be punished.

This message contradicted everything I had learned about the deep, rich tradition of Jewish forgiveness, good deeds, and repentance. It also reproduced the kind of anti-Semitism that had been used to justify the extermination of six million Jews in Europe during the Second World War. In our grade nine English class, there were children of Holocaust survivors. What we all needed to learn was how to critique Shakespeare's binary of Christian mercy and Jewish revenge, and how to respond to the xenophobic and anti-Semitic ideas and anti-Semitic talk in *The Merchant of Venice*.

Almost 30 years later, in the year 2000, I began writing *Lost Daughter,* which not only engages with the themes of Canadian xenophobia and anti-Semitism in the summer of 1933, but also portrays the rich tradition of forgiveness in Jewish thought and culture. In the summer of 2008, on the 75th anniversary of the Christie Pits riot, the play had its Canadian premiere as part of the Toronto Fringe Festival.

The title of the play comes from Jessica's last words to her Jewish father, Shylock, before her elopement with her Christian husband, Lorenzo in *The Merchant of Venice.*

> Farewell, and if my fortune be not crossed,
> I have a father, you a daughter, lost.

(Act 2, Scene V, lines 54-55)

Like Shakespeare's Jessica, my own Jessica begins the play as "a daughter lost". However, by the end of the play, she finds her place in ways that Shakespeare's Jessica does not.

CHARACTERS

JESSICA: A 19-year-old woman whose unknown past and dark looks make her seem exotic and mysterious to others. Born Jewish, she converted to Christianity when she eloped with Larry a year ago, and is still learning to fit into her new home in the Beaches.

LARRY: Jessica's husband, 22-years-old, boyish, outgoing, and affable. Unsettled before he met Jessica, Larry now feels rooted in his new home and family. He is currently unemployed and desperately searching for work.

BRADLEY: Larry's oldest and best friend, 22-years-old, an up-and-coming real estate agent living in his wife Pat's family home in the Beaches. Bradley is handsome, driven, and opinionated, but knows less than he would like to think.

PAT: Bradley's wife and a new mother, 22-years-old. Formerly a librarian, she walks and talks with confidence and authority and has taken Jessica under her wing.

ESTHER: Jessica's aunt, age 46, who owns and runs a boarding house in downtown Toronto. Having lost contact with Jessica for too many years, she is determined to establish a relationship with her.

SHIMON: Jessica's father, 53-years-old. An ambitious and successful manufacturer of ladies' dresses who has lost his business in the year since Jessica's elopement. A man who is burdened both by the loss of his daughter and by the loss of his business.

SETTING

The Beaches and Downtown Toronto
Summer 1933

At rise: There are two houses onstage. Jessica and Larry's house in the Beaches is set downstage right. The action in Jessica and Larry's house takes place outside on the porch of the house, which is filled with flowers planted in brightly coloured flowerpots. Esther's house in downtown Toronto is set downstage left. The action in Esther's house takes place inside in the dining room, which has a dining room table. Behind the two houses, there is a screen used for projecting slides.

ACT 1: LEAVING

Prelude

(A set of eight slides set to the first two minutes of "Kol Nidrei" (music that opens the Kol Nidre service that takes place the evening before Yom Kippur, the day of fasting and atonement for Jews) are projected onto the screen. The slides include the title and setting of the play [slide 1]; photographs of the boardwalk in the Beaches [slide 2]; a group of paddlers from the Balmy Beach Canoe Club [slide 3]; a group of Jews at a picnic at Kew Gardens in the Beaches [slide 4]; a wooden sign that says "Gentiles Only [slide 5]; two men, one wearing a swastika badge and the other wearing a swastika on his sweater [slide 6]; a sign saying "Hail Hitler" [sic] on the roof of the Christie Pits Club House [slide 7] and the boardwalk in the Beaches again [slide 8].)

(The photos in slides 2, 3 and 8 come from Barbaranne Boyer's *The Boardwalk Album: Memories of the Beach* [The Boston Mills Press, 1985]. The photos in slides 4-7 come from Cyril Levitt and William Shaffir's *The Riot at Christie Pits* [Lester and Orpen Dennys, 1987].

(In the 2008 Toronto Fringe Production, the following version of Kol Nidrei was used: Kol Nidrei Op. 47 from "A lasting Inspiration" by Jacqueline du Pre. EMI Records.)

(Just after sunset. ESTHER appears on stage during the first two minutes of "Kol Nidre" carrying two white candles and some matches. She walks into her dining room, places the candles in the silver candlesticks on the dining room table and lights the candles. The music ends.)

ESTHER

(Mournful, wistful) Leah. My darling, precious Leah. Happy Birthday. Forty-three. You would have been 43 years-old today. *(Pauses, wistful)* You'd be telling me about the wonderful new books Shimon and Jessica bought you for your birthday.
(ESTHER sighs heavily.)
I know, I know. I've been looking and looking. No one's seen her. Don't worry. I'll find her. I promise.

Scene 1

(Late afternoon. The front porch of JESSICA and LARRY's home. LARRY is putting a second coat of paint on the porch fence. There are piles of books surrounding one of the chairs on the porch. BRADLEY is sitting on the other porch chair.)

BRADLEY

(Reads from a letter he is holding) Conditions have become unbearable. People who live here have to go elsewhere to avoid the presence of undesirables. Local No. 5 of the Swastika Club has been formed in Kew Beach, and now has a membership of forty.

LARRY

Where did you say this was posted?

BRADLEY

On the bulletin board.

LARRY

(Skeptical) At the Balmy Beach Canoe Club.

BRADLEY

Yes. Stop interrupting and just listen. *(Continues reading)* Commencing Monday, July 31, our members will appear on the beaches, boardwalk, and in Kew Gardens wearing a nickel-plated badge with a swastika. *(Scans the letter quickly and continues to read)* All you are asked to do is buy an emblem and *wear* it. So, what do you think?

LARRY

They're exaggerating the problem.

BRADLEY

I bought us two badges.

LARRY

(Stops painting) What? From whom?

BRADLEY

Someone from the club. *(Takes the badges out of his pocket)* Here.

LARRY

(Starts painting again) No, thanks.

BRADLEY

Aren't you just a little upset at the truckloads of people who come on the weekends?

LARRY

It's a hot summer.

BRADLEY

And what about how dirty the beach is? Every Monday morning it takes a dozen men to clean it up.

LARRY
And by Monday afternoon, it's as clean as ever.

BRADLEY
No, it's not. It's swarming with flies. We never had flies until the beach was littered with garbage. And what about all the cars and trucks on the streets?

LARRY
They don't bother me. If I weren't lucky enough to live here, I'd come on the weekends too. Just like we did when we were kids.

BRADLEY
When we were kids, we took the streetcar. We didn't block people's driveways. Hey, stop painting for a minute and come and sit down.
(LARRY stops painting and sits down.)
There are folks from the Canoe Club who've bought badges. They'll be wearing the badges on the boardwalk and in the park. If you wear one, too, they'll see you as someone who wants to maintain the beauty of the Beach as much as they do. *(Beat)* These people have good jobs. Some of them work for the City. They might be able to find you a good job, too.

LARRY
So that's what this is about. Making a good impression on the fellows from the Canoe Club.

BRADLEY
What's wrong with making a good impression? I make a living selling real estate to the fellows at the Canoe Club. And *you* need a job. Jessica's money's almost gone, remember?
(LARRY bristles and goes back to painting the fence. BRAD follows him.)
Hey, everyone knows that dirty beaches don't sell houses. Neither do beaches with undesirables. All I want to do is keep Balmy Beach clean. Don't you?

LARRY

It wasn't that long ago that *we* were the undesirables.

BRADLEY

We were never undesirable. We spoke English. *(Angry)* And we followed the basic rules of decency. We never changed into our swimming suits in our cars. I don't like it, and I'm surprised to hear that it doesn't bother you at all. It's a mystery to me. Just like you getting married and not saying a word about it.

LARRY

(Puts down the paint brush) We've been through this before.

BRADLEY

There's something about Mystery Girl you don't want me to know.

LARRY

(Irritated) Her name is Jessica.

BRADLEY

What are you hiding?

LARRY

Nothing.

BRADLEY

We never used to have secrets. We always told each other everything.

LARRY

Look, we have the rest our lives for you and Jessica to get to know each other. She and Pat are already becoming friends. It's going to be fine. Everything's going to work out. I just need to find a job. Maybe something with numbers. I was always good with numbers.

> **BRADLEY**
> You need to join the Swastika Club.

> **LARRY**
> I don't want to –

> **PAT**
> *(From offstage)* Yoo-hoo. We're back.

> *(LARRY smiles and waves to JESSICA and PAT offstage.)*

> **BRADLEY**
> Come to one meeting. Listen to what the boys have to say. Then decide if you want to join or not. *(Urgent)* You've got to think of the house. You can't lose this house.

> **LARRY**
> *(Grim)* I know.

> *(LARRY comes off the porch to meet PAT and JESSICA who enter, pushing a baby carriage. BRADLEY returns to his seat on the porch.)*

> **LARRY**
> How was your walk?

> **JESSICA**
> Wonderful.

> **PAT**
> It's a little cooler on the boardwalk.

> **BRADLEY**
> Was it crowded?

PAT

Of course. It's Sunday. *(Gaily, but with an edge)* Not a picnic table to be had, not a word of English to be heard.

(BRADLEY laughs.)

PAT

(To LARRY) I hear *Jane Eyre* was a success.

LARRY

(Grins. Moves to take JESSICA's hand) It sure was.

PAT

(Dramatic) Jane Eyre. Full of trial and –

JESSICA

And tribulation, but in the end –

PAT

Love!

JESSICA

Marriage!

PAT and JESSICA

And a child!

BRADLEY

I can't believe you bought her another book.

LARRY

It's a paper gift. Pat told me I had to get something made out of paper for our first anniversary.

BRADLEY

But she hasn't even finished the ones she already has. How many books can one person read? Even you don't read that much.

PAT

(Insulted) Well, I *am* busy taking care of baby Emma all day.

BRADLEY

(Grins at LARRY) Reading anything longer than the front page and the sports section gives me a headache.

LARRY

(Grins back) And you're the one who married a librarian.

PAT

(Strategic) Speaking of which, Jessica and I have come up with plan. To help pay the mortgage.

BRADLEY

Pat!

LARRY

No, it's okay. What is it?

PAT

At the library, they're giving out a free card to anyone who's unemployed.

JESSICA

People are lining up to get in.

PAT

The permanent staff always goes on vacation in July and August, and I still know a number of the head librarians quite well. I'm sure that one of them could find Jessica a position, at least until the end of summer.

JESSICA

By then, you'll find a job.

BRADLEY

But she's married. You had to resign when you got married, remember?

PAT

She can say she's single. People won't know her at the children's library downtown.

LARRY

But wouldn't that be lying? And breaking the rules?

PAT

That particular rule was put in place to prevent two members of the same family from earning two salaries. You're not working.

BRADLEY

Maybe Larry should take the job.

PAT

(Lightly) Jessica's the reader in the family.

(LARRY nods.)

LARRY

(To JESSICA) So, what do you think?

JESSICA

I think it's the perfect job for me.

Scene 2

(Late afternoon. JESSICA is on the porch, taking the dead leaves off the flowers in the flowerpots. ESTHER enters and stands at the bottom of the porch stairs. She is carrying a large black purse and a cloth shopping bag. She is uncomfortable and looks up and down the street to see if anyone else is out on the porch. Finally she gathers up her courage and calls out to JESSICA.)

65

ESTHER

(Too loud) Good afternoon!

JESSICA

Oh! *(Turns around to face ESTHER)* You startled me. I didn't hear you coming up the street.

ESTHER

(Softer) I'm sorry. I didn't mean to scare you.

JESSICA

(Recovers) That's all right. Can I help you?

ESTHER

You're the new librarian at the children's library, aren't you?

JESSICA

(Surprised) Yes.

ESTHER

I've heard you read during storytelling. You read beautifully.

JESSICA

Thank you. *(Beat)* I recognize you now. You've been at storytelling every day this week. I don't usually see too many adults.

ESTHER

Ben told me about it. His family lives in my boarding house.

JESSICA

Oh, Ben!

ESTHER

He thinks the world of you. *(Beat)* Have you lived here long?

JESSICA

Just over a year.

ESTHER

It's a long trip to the library by streetcar.

JESSICA

Yes it is. How long have you lived here?

ESTHER

Oh, I don't live in this neighbourhood.

JESSICA

Then how did you find me?

ESTHER

(Reluctant) I followed you home on the streetcar.

JESSICA

You followed me home?

ESTHER

(Quickly) I hope you don't mind. I didn't want to disturb you at work. I wanted to talk to you in private.

JESSICA

Talk to me about what?

ESTHER

My sister. You look just like her. And you have her daughter's name. Jessica.

JESSICA

What?

ESTHER

It sounds crazy, I know. But I think you may be my sister's daughter, Jessica. I may be your aunt.

JESSICA

I'm sorry, Mrs. ...?

ESTHER

Call me Esther.

JESSICA

You're mistaken. My mother didn't have a sister.

ESTHER

What was your mother's name? Was it Leah?

> *(ESTHER reaches into her purse and takes out a photograph.)*

Here, look at this. It's a photograph of Leah on her wedding day. Does my Leah look like your mother?

> *(JESSICA takes a look at the photograph, doesn't answer, and hands it back)*

ESTHER

(Excited) Her hair is all done up here. Leah had very long hair. Did your mother have long hair?

JESSICA

(Looks at her watch) I'm sorry, but it's quite late. I have to begin dinner. Good-bye.

> *(Turns around, opens the screen door and walks into the house.)*

ESTHER

(Through the screen door) Please. Don't walk away. I've waited so many years to talk to you.

> *(JESSICA reluctantly stops, turns around and comes back outside.)*

Tell me what you remember about your mother.

JESSICA

I don't remember anything.

ESTHER

Then tell me what you've been told about her.

JESSICA

She died when I was very small.

ESTHER

(Nods) Yes. Yes. You were three years-old.
  (JESSICA moves a step closer to ESTHER.)
  Your father raised you.

JESSICA

(Stiffens) It's late. My husband will be home any moment.

ESTHER

(Loud and excited) You're married!

  *(JESSICA looks up and down the street to see if anyone is
  listening to the conversation.)*

JESSICA

(Softer than ESTHER, trying to get ESTHER to lower her voice) Yes.
But this really isn't a good time to talk.

ESTHER

(Looks down the street, softer) I understand. *(Looks at JESSICA)* I'll
come back to the library next week. We can talk some more then.

Scene 3

  *(Morning. PAT is visiting JESSICA, who is watering the
  flowers on the porch.)*

PAT

Be careful. You don't want to give that one too much water.

JESSICA

(Gives the plant she's about to water just a bit of water) How's that?

PAT

Perfect. *(Beat)* I hear someone followed you home yesterday.

JESSICA

What? Who told you that?

PAT

One of the neighbours.
(Waits for JESSICA to respond. JESSICA focuses her concentration on watering the next pot of flowers.)
(Impatient) So, who is she?

JESSICA

(Continues watering, as casual as she can muster) A long-lost aunt.

PAT

(Extremely interested) Really?

JESSICA

(Casual) Yes.

PAT

How exciting. How did she find you?

JESSICA

(Careful) She recognized me during storytelling at the library. How much water does this one get?

PAT

Lots. It needs to be kept moist.
(JESSICA gives the plant a lot of water.)
How did she know to look for you at the library?

JESSICA

I don't know.

PAT

A mystery. So, are you going to see her again?

JESSICA

I hope not.

PAT

(Surprised) Why? Aren't you curious? To hear what she has to say about your mother?

JESSICA

Yes, of course. But if I become too friendly with her, she might tell my father where I'm living.

PAT

He doesn't know?

JESSICA

(Sorry that she has said as much as she has) No.

PAT

Why not?

JESSICA

(Starts watering another plant) It's a long story.

PAT

I want to hear it.

JESSICA

It's really not that interesting.

PAT

It is to me.
(JESSICA is silent and continues to water the flowers.)
You know, the secret of a good friendship is that there are no secrets in a good friendship.

JESSICA

(Stops watering, feeling pressured) What do you want to know?

PAT

(Eager) Well, I've always wondered how you and Larry met. He never told us.

JESSICA

We met at my father's dress factory.

PAT

(Surprised) Dress factory? Where?

JESSICA

(Hesitates) Where?

PAT

Where was the factory?

JESSICA

(Holds PAT's gaze) Dundas and Spadina.

PAT

Oh! You're a Jew?

JESSICA

(Quickly) No. Not any more. A minister married us. I'm Protestant now. *(Beat)* You have to promise me that you won't tell any of this to Bradley. Larry asked me not to talk about ... my past.

PAT

(Nods) I see. It all makes sense now.

JESSICA

What?

PAT

Why Larry didn't talk about you. Larry talks to Bradley about everything. *(Beat)* Everything, except you.

JESSICA

(Attempts a light tone) I didn't know that Larry talked to Bradley about everything.

PAT

They're very close. *(Lowers her voice, confidential)* The summer Larry's father died, his mother was inconsolable. She wouldn't get out of bed. Larry spent most of his days and nights with Bradley. They'd take the streetcar out here and go swimming. Larry didn't have any money, so Bradley paid for his carfare. Imagine losing your father at thirteen and your mother at fifteen.

JESSICA

(Nods) Terrible.

PAT

But now he has you. *(Prompts)* So, you were working in your father's factory.

JESSICA

I was the bookkeeper. *(Puts down the watering can)* I wanted to go to university, but my father said that I should use my brains to work for him. He taught me how to do the books himself. I worked in a tiny office in a corner of the factory. Six days a week.

PAT

What did you do for fun?

JESSICA

I read. I went to the library every Thursday to take out books for the week. *(Grins)* The librarian helped me choose them.

PAT

Didn't you have any friends?

JESSICA

Not really. The few friends I made in high school drifted away after we graduated.

PAT

It sounds dreary.

> *(JESSICA doesn't answer. She picks up the watering can and starts watering another plant.)*

So how did you and Larry meet?

JESSICA

(Puts down the watering can) Larry delivered fabric to the factory. He had to come into the office to get the delivery bill signed. It only took a second to sign the bill, but Larry would stay for a few minutes and try to make me laugh. He once told me that I had the nicest laugh, but that he didn't think that I laughed very much. He thought I was very sad. He could see it in my eyes.

PAT

It's hard to imagine. *(Teases)* All I see is love in those eyes.

JESSICA

(Laughs and picks up one of the small flowerpots) Anyway, Larry made his delivery on Tuesdays. I began wearing my nicest clothes to work on Tuesdays. My light blue sweater with the pearl buttons.

PAT

Blue is a good colour. Not too loud.

JESSICA

Tuesday was the only day of the week I didn't mind going to the factory. On all the other days, I hated it. It was noisy. The sewing machines were so loud the women had to shout at each other. Some days, I could hardly hear myself think. I needed to check my figures three or four times to make sure that I didn't make a mistake. *(Pauses)* When he found a mistake in the figures, my father got excited and raised his voice. That voice was ugly and it made me nauseous inside. The hardest days were the rainy days. The factory was cold and damp and I couldn't wait to leave. Larry's visits got longer and longer. Then one day, he bought me a present. A book.

PAT

(Excited) Romeo and Juliet. I was the one who suggested it.

74

JESSICA

(Smiles) Romeo and Juliet. My father walked into the office to see if there was a problem. Larry had been in the office for a long time. When he saw the book, he was furious. He called Larry's boss and said he wanted him transferred to another delivery route. *(Angry)* Larry lost his job. Because of my father. *(Beat)* We began meeting secretly. Then, we decided to elope. I wrote my father a letter and left it on my desk in the office. Then I took some money and my mother's turquoise ring.

PAT

The money for the house. You stole it from your father?

JESSICA

(Indignant, defensive) I didn't steal it. I took exactly what he would have paid Mrs. Goldberg for four years of housekeeping if she hadn't retired and I hadn't taken over. I took that and exactly what he would have paid a bookkeeper for the last year, if he had had to hire one.

PAT

But the ring –

JESSICA

I inherited the ring from my mother. My father was to give it to me on the day my first baby is born.

PAT

(Nods slowly) No wonder you're not in contact. Was it difficult? Becoming Protestant?

JESSICA

No. Do you know what kind of lives Jews have? Lives of trouble. *(With increasing emotion)* In Russia, pogroms. In Canada, getting beaten up, and long hours in a damp, cold factory. I don't want that kind of life.

(JESSICA throws the flowerpot she is holding onto the ground, where it shatters. Startled, PAT jumps at the sudden crash.)

(Looks at the shattered flowerpot on the ground, upset) Oh. I hope I didn't wake the baby. What a mess. I'll go get the broom.

PAT

(Regains her composure) No. It's almost time for you to go to work. You go get ready. I'll get the broom.

JESSICA

(Bitter, wistful, grateful all at once) If I was still Jewish, I couldn't work at the library.

PAT

So it's a good thing you're not. Go get ready.

JESSICA

(Looks down at the mess) I'm sorry.

PAT

Don't worry. It's only a little dirt. I'll clean it up.

(JESSICA and PAT exit into the house. Lights dim on the porch and come up on the dining room where ESTHER is vigorously polishing a pair of silver candlesticks on her dining room table. In this split-scene PAT re-enters onto the porch and sweeps up the dirt during ESTHER's monologue. When she is finished, PAT exits into the house.)

ESTHER

Leah, I found her! And I spoke to her! She's all grown up now. She's lovely, Leah, just lovely. She looks so much like you. And the children at the library just adore her. With me, she's a little reserved. But that's to be expected. She hasn't seen me in sixteen years. *(Beat)* One thing I found strange. She's living outside the city. Why she wants to live there, I don't know. Such a long ride to the library. And

I didn't see too many Jews there. *(Beat)* No, she's fine, Leah. You worry too much. All right, all right, I'll find out if anything's wrong. I'll invite her over for tea. *(Beat)* Of course, she'll come. When I tell her that I want to give her your beautiful candlesticks as a wedding present, she'll come. *(Beat)* If she doesn't want to come, I'll take the streetcar home with her. There's plenty of time to talk. It's a half-hour ride to the Beach. A hot half-hour ride – not that I'm complaining. Don't worry. I'll find out what's what. I promise you.

Scene 4

(Night. LARRY is watching JESSICA lighting two white candles on the porch. When the candles have been lit, JESSICA sits close to LARRY and takes his hand. The porch is lit only by the candlelight emanating from the candles on the table.)

LARRY
This is very nice. Very romantic.

JESSICA
(Looks up) Look at all those stars.
(LARRY looks up.)
When I was little, I used to look up in the sky and pretend that the brightest star in the sky was my mother and that she was looking down at me. And then I'd tell her whatever it was that was on my mind. Sometimes it was good news. Like when I'd do well on a test at school.

LARRY
And sometimes it was bad news.

JESSICA
Yes.

LARRY
(Teases) Did she ever talk back?

JESSICA

(Serious) Sometimes. She would never answer any of my questions, but she would sometimes tell me what to do.

LARRY

You mean, she'd give you advice?

JESSICA

Not advice as much as commands. Maybe, not commands. More like directions.

LARRY

Like what?

JESSICA

Study harder. Read more books.

LARRY

She must be pleased. No one reads more books than you. *(Beat)* If you were talking to her tonight, what would you say?

JESSICA

I'd tell her how happy I am to be married to you, how much I love you, how much I love our home, and …

LARRY

And?

JESSICA

And I'm going to have a baby.

LARRY

What?

JESSICA

I'm going to have a baby.

LARRY

When?

JESSICA

In January.

LARRY

I'm going to be a father?

JESSICA

(Laughs) Yes.

LARRY

(Stands up, lifts her off the chair, swings her around, then puts her down and hugs her) I'm going to be a father! We're going to have a baby.

JESSICA

(Hugs him back, laughs) Yes, yes. *(Beat)* So you're not worried?

LARRY

(Releases JESSICA from his hug so he can see her face) Worried?

JESSICA

About being able to pay for the doctor and the hospital and –

LARRY

I'll find something soon. *(Grins)* I've always wanted a lot of children.

JESSICA

(Laughs) How many?

LARRY

Four.

JESSICA

Then we'll have four. After you get a steady job.

LARRY

(Kisses her deeply) I love you so much.

JESSICA

(Moved) And I love you.

LARRY

(Strokes her hair) Come sit down.
    (They sit down.)
We've come a long way, haven't we? A year ago, we were meeting secretly at Christie Pits. And now we're going to have a baby. *(Shakes his head in disbelief.)* We're going to have a baby.

JESSICA

In seven-and-a-half months. I'll have to leave the library.

LARRY

When?

JESSICA

In about six weeks.

LARRY

I'll find something by then.

JESSICA

(Touches his cheek) There's something I want to show you.

LARRY

(Strokes her hair) What?
    (JESSICA reaches into her pocket and pulls out a small box. She opens the box carefully and takes out the turquoise ring.)

JESSICA

(Hands the ring to LARRY) This.

LARRY

(Takes the ring) It's a ring.

JESSICA

Turquoise. It belonged to my mother. My father was to give it to me on the day my first baby was born. Would you put it on *(looks at both her hands)* my right hand?

LARRY

Don't you want to wait until the baby is born?

JESSICA

No. I want to share this moment with my mother.

LARRY

All right. What was your mother's name? I forget.

JESSICA

(A little disappointed that he doesn't remember) Leah.

LARRY

(Remembers) Leah. *(Looks up at the brightest star)* Leah, Jessica and I have wonderful news to share with you. We're going to have our first child.

> *(LARRY slips the ring onto the third finger of JESSICA'S right hand. She holds up her hand to admire the ring.)*

JESSICA

(Soft) Mazel Tov.

LARRY

What?

JESSICA

Nothing. *(Takes LARRY's hand and laughs)* I'm very happy. Very, very happy.

LARRY

Me, too. So much has changed since I met you. I have a home. A wife. A baby.

81

(LARRY suddenly lets go of JESSICA's hand, gets up and paces back and forth.)

Jess, I promise you – we won't lose this house.

JESSICA

(Tries to be reassuring) Of course we won't. You've been out looking for work all day, every day, for months. Something will come up.

(LARRY stops pacing.)

LARRY

You're right. Something has to come up.

Scene 5

(Later that night. LARRY and BRADLEY are sitting on the porch, which is now lit by moonlight.)

BRADLEY

I thought you didn't want to join.

LARRY

Jessica's going to have a baby.

BRADLEY

What?

LARRY

Jessica's going to –

BRADLEY

Congratulations.

(He leans over and slaps LARRY on the back.)

LARRY

(Grins) Thank you.

BRADLEY

Our kids will grow up together. Just like we did.

LARRY

(Laughs) Now, there's trouble coming to the Beach. *(Sober)* The baby changes everything. I need to do whatever it takes to find a job.

BRADLEY

(Hits LARRY on the shoulder) Right.

LARRY

These are tough times. I need to meet people who can find me a job. A decent-paying job. A job with the City. *(Beat)* And I *do* want to keep our beaches clean.

BRADLEY

Of course you do. You live here.

LARRY

(Struggles) But, they *are* public beaches. It's wrong to keep people out.

BRADLEY

No, it's not. Not when they don't follow the basic rules of decency.

LARRY

Like what?

BRADLEY

Like changing their babies' diapers on the picnic tables. Who wants to eat off a picnic table after that?

LARRY

Don't you and Pat bring a tablecloth?

BRADLEY

Yes, but that's not the point. The point is decent people don't –

LARRY

I know what the point is. Has there been any fighting?

BRADLEY

Some.

LARRY

I don't like fighting.

BRADLEY

The Jews always start it. We have to fight back.
(LARRY is silent.)
There's nothing wrong in defending yourself.

LARRY

No. I guess there isn't.

BRADLEY

So should I tell the boys we have a new member?
(LARRY nods.)
I'll introduce you to everyone at the next meeting.
(BRADLEY takes a swastika badge out of his pocket and pins it onto LARRY's shirt.)
Here's your badge.
(LARRY is embarrassed.)
Hey. *(Takes a piece of paper out of his back pocket)* I have something to show you.

LARRY

What is it?

BRADLEY

It's a song. One of the boys wrote it. We're going to sing it the next time we march along the boardwalk.
(BRADLEY stands up and sings the following words to the tune of "Home on the Range")
"O give me a home, where the Gentiles may roam,
Where the Jews are not rampant all day.

(Looks up from his song sheet) Pretty clever, eh?

"Where seldom is heard a loud Jewish word
And the Gentiles are free all the day."

(BRADLEY laughs. LARRY looks out at the street.)

BRADLEY
(Sits down again) Now, I'll teach you the words. You know the tune.

Scene 6

(Late afternoon. ESTHER is sitting on the porch. Her purse and shopping bag are beside her chair. JESSICA enters with two glasses of iced tea.)

ESTHER
(Takes the glass JESSICA offers, grateful) Thank you. *(Takes a sip of iced tea)* Such a hot ride. So, you'll accept Leah's silver candlesticks as a wedding gift?

JESSICA
I would love to have them.

ESTHER
(Very pleased) Good. I'll bring them over to the library.

JESSICA
That's very kind of you.

ESTHER
My pleasure. Tell me, did you and Shimon light candles on Friday night?

JESSICA
I did, but not my father. After my mother died, it made him too sad. So, I lit the candles while he was at work. They'd be out before he

got home. When I was little, I used to close my eyes, look into the flame of the candles and try to see my mother's face.

ESTHER

(Moved) Well, this Friday night you can light your mother's candlesticks.
>*(JESSICA is silent.)*

You don't light candles anymore, do you?
>*(JESSICA shakes her head)*

Your husband isn't Jewish.

JESSICA

No.

ESTHER

As long as he's a good man, that's what counts.

JESSICA

Larry's a very good man.

ESTHER

(Nods) I'm glad to hear it. *(Smiles)* I see you're wearing your mother's ring.

JESSICA

Yes.

ESTHER

Shimon gave you the ring?

JESSICA

(Stiffens) It was my mother's wish that I have it when …

ESTHER

(Soft) When you gave birth to your first child. *(Loud)* You're pregnant!

JESSICA

(Surprised and embarrassed) Yes. But it's still a secret.

ESTHER

So who would I tell?

JESSICA

No one, I hope.

ESTHER

So, when is my grandniece expected?

JESSICA

January.

ESTHER

A New Year's baby. How I wish your mother – May She Rest in Peace – were here.

JESSICA

Esther, tell me how my mother died.

ESTHER

Shimon never told you?

JESSICA

No.

ESTHER

(Sits back in her chair) Not long after your third birthday, Leah began to fall sick. But she didn't say anything. Not to me. Not to your father. Both of us were working long hours at the factory, and she didn't want to worry us.

JESSICA

You worked in my father's factory?

ESTHER

Yes, but he didn't own it then. We were working for someone else, and Shimon was saving to go into business for himself. Anyway, one day I was visiting Leah and you. She seemed pale, and I thought she was getting too thin. I insisted she go see a doctor. I made the appointment for Leah. And then, when she needed to see a specialist, I made that appointment too. But by then, *(shakes her head)* she was so eaten up by the cancer that there was nothing anyone could do.

(JESSICA opens her mouth and covers her mouth with her hand.)

There was almost no time to say goodbye. I was very angry. *(Pause)* And I made a terrible mistake.

JESSICA

What did you do?

ESTHER

It's what I said. *(Sighs)* You have to understand. I was very, very upset. Leah was my sister and my best friend. After the *Shiva*, Shimon and I went back to work. Our first day back, the boss asked us to do a double shift. I said no, but Shimon said yes. And that made me angry. I yelled at him in front of all the workers. And I said some terrible things.

JESSICA

What? What did you say?

ESTHER

I told him if he had paid more attention to Leah instead of working double shifts, maybe he would have noticed how ill she was. Maybe he would have insisted she see a doctor. I lost control. I began to shout at him. "If you had paid more attention to your wife, then she would be alive today."

(ESTHER puts her face in her hands.)

(Looks up) I accused him of murdering her.

(JESSICA gasps.)

Of course, he began to shout back at me. "Get out of here. Go home. And don't ever talk to me again."

JESSICA

(Horrified) What did you do?

ESTHER

What could I do? I went home.

JESSICA

Did you try to talk to him?

ESTHER

Of course. But he wouldn't talk back. And he wouldn't let me see you either. *(Sighs)* He gave Mrs. Goldberg strict instructions not to let me visit. But I came anyway and begged her to let me take you to the park.

JESSICA

You took me to the park? I don't remember.

ESTHER

You were only three. On nice days, we went to the park and on rainy days, we went to the library. For six months, I visited you secretly. Once a week. Then, your father found out. He told Mrs. Goldberg that if she let me take you out again, he would fire her. Mrs. Goldberg was a widow. She needed the job to live. And you had just lost your mother. So I stopped coming. But I also kept trying to change Shimon's mind. Every New Year, just before *Yom Kippur,* I went to see him and asked for forgiveness. Every year, he refused. He's a stubborn man, your father.
    (JESSICA nods.)
I decided to find you when you turned eighteen. I heard you went to work at Shimon's factory. I knew you finished at the same time everyday. One o'clock. On the day of your eighteenth birthday, I went to the factory, planning to follow you home. I waited outside

the factory. But you didn't come out. I waited until two. Until three. You didn't come out. I thought that maybe you were sick, so –

JESSICA

I left the day before my eighteenth birthday. Larry and I got married the day after.

ESTHER

(Nods) So, I began looking for you all over again. But no one had seen you. Until one day, Ben came home and told me about the beautiful new lady at the library who looked just like my sister. Her name was Jessica.

JESSICA

How did he know what my mother looked like?

ESTHER

He had seen Leah's photograph in the living room. And, of course, he knew I had been looking for you. Everyone did. The next day, I went to storytelling with him. The rest of the story, you know.

JESSICA

The rest of the story I know.

ESTHER

(Tentatively takes JESSICA's hand) Now, you are a married woman and you're going to have a baby. Your mother – may she rest in peace – would be so proud.

JESSICA

You think so?

ESTHER

Of course. Why wouldn't she be?

JESSICA

I dreamt of *Mama* last night. And in the dream, she was angry.

ESTHER

About what?

JESSICA

Because I was wearing her turquoise ring. She said something to me in Hebrew. I think it was Hebrew.

ESTHER

What did she say?

JESSICA

It sounded like *(tentative)* "*s'lichah*".

ESTHER

(Pronouncing it with confidence) S'lichah.

JESSICA

Yes. What does it mean?

ESTHER

Forgiveness. It means forgiveness. *(Beat)* Your mother thinks you need to ask for forgiveness.
   (JESSICA is silent.)
   You know, she tells me what to do, too.

JESSICA

She does?

ESTHER

First she wanted me to find you. Now she wants me to keep you safe.

JESSICA

Safe? *(Laughs)* I'm not in any trouble.

ESTHER

The world is a dangerous place. Especially for Jews.

JESSICA

But I'm not …

ESTHER

Haven't you been reading the papers? There's going to be a pogrom.

JESSICA

(In disbelief) A pogrom. Where?

ESTHER

In Germany. I was reading about it this morning. In the Jewish paper. *(Goes into her shopping bag and finds the newspaper)* Here. You don't read the Jewish paper?

JESSICA

No. I don't read Yiddish.

ESTHER

Can you understand it?

JESSICA

Just a few words.

ESTHER

Then, I'll translate it for you. The headline says, "God Says 'Kill Off The Jews': Nazis Openly Call For Pogroms. Jews Are Not Humans."

JESSICA

Who –

ESTHER

It's from a leaflet that was distributed in Berlin. Hitler and his Nazis want to kill all the Jews in Germany.

JESSICA

I don't believe it. There wasn't any news of this in *The Telegram*.

ESTHER

The English newspapers don't write about what's happening to the Jews in Germany. Listen to this. *(Translates from the paper)* "There are two kinds of anti-Semitism. One of a high kind, it limits Jewish power through laws. The other, baser sort, kills Jews –

JESSICA

It says this in the leaflet?

ESTHER

Yes. *(Continues reading)* "The latter is perhaps a dreadful kind, but it brings the best results because it ends for a time the Jewish question by exterminating them."

Scene 7

> *(Early evening. LARRY is sitting on the porch. BRADLEY enters wearing his swastika badge.)*

BRADLEY

(Looks at his watch, excited.) Are you ready? It's almost time to meet the boys.

LARRY

You go ahead. I want to say hello to Jessica before going.

BRADLEY

"No, I'll wait for you. Where's your badge? You need to put your badge on."

> (LARRY takes the badge out of his pocket and pins it onto his shirt. BRADLEY begins pacing.)

Where is she? We don't want to be late. It's better to be walking at the front of the line.

LARRY

I don't care where I walk.

                    BRADLEY

Well, I do, and I want you walking next to me. In case there's any
trouble.

                    LARRY

I gotta be honest with you. I don't like parading along the boardwalk.
It just doesn't feel right.

                    BRADLEY

Just stay close to me and –
          (He sees JESSICA approaching.)
Hey, here she comes.
          *(LARRY stands up and waves as JESSICA enters carrying the
          silver candlesticks in a velvet bag like a baby. LARRY goes to
          greet JESSICA and takes the bag. The bag covers up his
          badge. They walk up to the porch.)*
Hi, Jessie. What's in the bag?

                    JESSICA

A gift. *(Looks up at BRADLEY's shirt.)* What's that on your shirt?

                    BRADLEY

My swastika badge. We're protesting the disfiguring of our beaches.

          *(Larry puts the bag with the candlesticks down on the porch
          table, revealing his badge.)*

                    JESSICA

(Looks at LARRY's shirt) You're wearing one, too!

                    LARRY

(Uncomfortable) Yes.

                    JESSICA

(Surprised, sharp) The swastika is a Nazi emblem.

BRADLEY

Our Club isn't connected to any Nazi organizations.

JESSICA

But, you're wearing the badges to intimidate people. That's what they use the badges for in Germany. You've read about what's happening in Germany. They're burning books, arresting and beating people –

BRADLEY

(Getting angry) And I told you we're not connected to any Nazis.

LARRY

(Takes JESSICA's hand) If Bradley says the club isn't connected to any Nazi organizations, then I'm sure it's not.

JESSICA

(Takes her hand away) Do you really think that people wearing a badge like that don't mean any harm?

LARRY

(Uneasy) All they want to do is keep the beach clean.

BRADLEY

(Looks at his watch) It's time to go. Are you coming?

LARRY

I'll meet you there.

BRADLEY

Okay. Don't be too long.

    (BRADLEY exits.)

JESSICA

(Upset) Take it off. Please, take it off.

(LARRY takes off the badge.)

LARRY

Okay, okay, it's off.

JESSICA

I don't want to see it on you again. When did you get it?

LARRY

Yesterday.

JESSICA

(Incredulous) Why did you agree to wear a badge like that?

LARRY

There are people in the Club who work for the City. Bradley said that if I joined the Club, they could help me find a job.

> *(JESSICA shakes her head in disapproval. LARRY becomes angry, raising his voice.)*

Well, I have to do something, don't I? I've been out all day, every day for a year, looking for a decent job. There isn't anything out there. I'm only trying to save my house.

JESSICA

(Upset) Your house? It's not just your house. It's our house. Who paid for the down payment? Me. Whose salary is paying the mortgage? Mine.

LARRY

(Very upset) Very soon, you won't be able to pay for anything. Then what we are going to do? I don't care about how I find a job.

JESSICA

(Also very upset) I care! People who wear swastikas in Germany want to kill off the Jews.

LARRY

What are you saying? That I want to kill off the Jews who come to Kew Beach? If that's what you think, then you shouldn't have married me.

JESSICA

When I married you, there was never any talk about "dirty Jews" on the beach.
Now –

LARRY

When I married *you*, you never talked about Jews either. All you talked about was leaving. Leaving the factory, leaving your father –

JESSICA

(Close to tears) Just because –

LARRY

You wanted to leave it all behind. And you did. You left it all behind. This is our home now, and I'm not going to lose it.

> *(LARRY storms offstage.)*

JESSICA

(Close to tears) They're planning to kill all the Jews.

End of Act 1

ACT 2: RETURNING

Scene 1

> *(Late afternoon. ESTHER's dining room, where ESTHER is looking through a box of photographs. ESTHER looks up and sees SHIMON standing at the entrance of the room.)*

> ### ESTHER
> *(Shocked, stands up)* Shimon!

> ### SHIMON
> *(Uncomfortable)* Hello, Esther. I'm not interrupting you? One of the boarders let me in. A young boy.

> ### ESTHER
> Ben.

> ### SHIMON
> He told me you were here.

> ### ESTHER
> And here I am. Do you want to sit down?

> ### SHIMON
> Thank you.

> ### ESTHER
> Be careful. One of the legs on that chair is loose. On this one, too.

> > *(SHIMON sits down carefully, takes a handkerchief out of a pocket and wipes the back of his neck. ESTHER also sits down carefully.)*

> ### SHIMON
> Why don't you get the chairs fixed?

> ### ESTHER
> I don't see you for ten years, and the first thing say is 'why don't I get the chairs fixed?'

> ### SHIMON
> *(Puts the handkerchief back into his pocket and shakes his head)* Ten years. It's been a long time.

ESTHER

I'm surprised to see you.

SHIMON

(Nods) I need your help.

ESTHER

(Cool) My help?

SHIMON

Leah told me to come and ask you for help.

ESTHER

Leah?

SHIMON

She spoke to me last night. The first time in sixteen years.

ESTHER

And she told you to come to see me.

SHIMON

She said you would help me find Jessica. Maybe you heard? Jessica left home. A year ago. She married a *goy* and I have no idea where she is. Leah told me that you were looking for her, too.

ESTHER

(Angry) You need Leah to tell you I've been looking for Jessica? For how many years did I come to you and beg you to see her? How many years? She was my only niece. My only tie to Leah. And now that you've lost her, too, you want me to help you look for her? *(Incredulous)* I should forgive you after you refused to forgive me, and we should look for Jessica together?
    (ESTHER stands up.)
(Angry) All those years. Gone. And now you want my help?

SHIMON

(Stands up, also angry) You called me a murderer.

    (ESTHER is silent.)

You never thought I was good enough for Leah. You wanted her to marry someone younger. A writer or a teacher. I worked in the *schmatta* business, just like you. *(Beat)* I was afraid you'd turn Jessica against me. Please … She's the only family I have left. Now she's gone. *(With dignity)* Have some compassion for a lonely father.

ESTHER

Like you had compassion for a lonely aunt?

SHIMON

All right. All right. I made a mistake. Every day, I wake up in my empty house, without her –

ESTHER

Like me. Just like me.

SHIMON

(Pauses) All right. Yes. Just like you. *(Beat, then with courage)* I've come to ask for forgiveness. To make amends. I don't know how. I don't have much anymore. I lost the factory, but –

ESTHER

(Surprised) You lost the factory? But it was so busy. You had so many customers.

SHIMON

Times are bad. Lots of them went out of business. I couldn't make payroll. So, I sold everything to pay the workers what I owed them. They came and took away the sewing machines, the buttons, the thread … *(Sad)* The little desk I bought Jessica when she came to do the bookkeeping.

ESTHER

So, how are you living?

SHIMON

The house is paid off, thank God, and I do some tailoring from home.

ESTHER

You have no savings?

SHIMON

No.

ESTHER

What happened to your money? Gambling?

SHIMON

(Angry) No, not gambling. *(Pause)* Jessica took the money.

ESTHER

(Shocked) Jessica? I don't believe it.

SHIMON

(Sighs) The year she worked for me, I didn't pay her a salary. She didn't need one. I paid all her expenses. Books, clothes, carfare. More books. When she left, she took the money and Leah's turquoise ring. It wasn't a lot of money, but it was all that I had. Everything else went into the business.

(SHIMON takes out his handkerchief and wipes his forehead again.)

ESTHER

You must be mad at her.

SHIMON

(Wipes the back of his neck) No.

ESTHER

(Insists) You're not mad her for taking your money?

101

SHIMON

(Caught, raises his voice) All right. Yes. I'm mad. But what's done is done. *(Struggles to lower his voice)* I want to find her. I need your help.

ESTHER

She's been gone a year. Why all of sudden do you want her back?

SHIMON

I miss her.

ESTHER

You didn't miss her before?

SHIMON

The day she left, I was furious. I locked the door to her room and tried to forget about her. I had to work like a dog to keep the business going. But then, I lost the business. Tailoring isn't enough to live on. So I decided to rent out her room. When I unlocked the door, I found a picture. Leah and I, on our wedding day. I don't know where she got it. I didn't give it to her. I locked up all the pictures when Leah died. I haven't seen that picture in sixteen years. I couldn't put it down. That's when Leah spoke to me. That's when she told me to go see you. Esther, I want to talk to her. *(Beat)* Maybe there's something I can do to help you.

ESTHER

(Furious) You know when I needed your help? After Leah died. I promised to be a mother to her daughter. That's when I needed your help. To keep my promise to Leah.

SHIMON

Forgive me, Esther. I was wrong.
    (ESTHER doesn't respond.)
Help me find her. Please. These are dangerous times for Jews, and I don't know where she is.

ESTHER

(Pauses) (Reluctant) All right.

SHIMON

(Surprised) All right?

ESTHER

Yes. *(Beat)* And there is something you can do to help me.

SHIMON

What is it?

ESTHER

Ben, the boy who let you in. His father is also a tailor. His wife died a year ago, and he has a family of five to feed. If you have a little extra work some week –

SHIMON

(Quickly) I have some this week. He can come back to the house with me.

ESTHER

All right. He'll go with you, and I'll look for Jessica.

Scene 2

(Late afternoon. JESSICA and PAT, sitting on the porch.)

PAT

We missed you at the picnic last weekend. Larry said you needed to rest.

JESSICA

Did he?

PAT

I know why you stayed home.

JESSICA

(Surprised) You do?

PAT

(Grabs JESSICA's hand) The baby.

JESSICA

What?

PAT

(Squeezes JESSICA's hand) The baby!

JESSICA

You know about the baby?

PAT

Bradley told me. *(Hurt)* But I would have preferred to hear it from you.

JESSICA

(Sincere, taking PAT's hand in both of hers) I'm sorry. I didn't think Larry would tell Bradley about the baby before I had a chance to tell you.

PAT

Larry tells Bradley everything, remember?

JESSICA

(Let's go of PAT's hand) I'm sorry.

PAT

I forgive you. *(Beat)* What's wrong? You don't seem very excited.

JESSICA

I'm worried. Larry needs to find a job before I have to leave the library.

PAT

Bradley thinks that someone from the Club will come through with a job.

JESSICA

Which club? The Canoe Club or the Swastika Club?

PAT

I really don't understand why you object to Larry joining Bradley on the boardwalk. There's nothing wrong with wanting our Sundays to be free from the crowds who come up here every weekend.
(JESSICA doesn't respond.)
Some of those people are extremely rude. *(Beat)* People living in the Beach have just as much right to organize and demonstrate to keep our neighbourhood clean as the Jews downtown who stand outside Queen's Park to condemn Hitler.

JESSICA

People who come to the Beach on the weekends leave orange peels on the sand. Hitler is talking about killing the Jews in Germany.

PAT

Where did you hear that Hitler is talking about killing Jews?

JESSICA

In the Jewish newspaper.

PAT

It sounds like an exaggeration to me. *(Beat)* I didn't know that you read the Jewish newspaper.

JESSICA

I don't, but my aunt does.

PAT

You mean that woman who followed you home?

JESSICA

Yes.

PAT

You've been talking to her?

JESSICA

(Careful) Yes. At the library. *(Excited)* She brought me a wedding present. Silver candlesticks. They belonged to my mother.

PAT

Why didn't you tell me?

JESSICA

I was just about to. Wait a minute. I'll bring them out.

(She stands up to go inside.)

PAT

I hope you're not becoming too friendly with this woman.

JESSICA

What do you mean?

PAT

You don't want her coming to visit here. Nobody here knows you were born Jewish. Not even Bradley.
    (JESSICA doesn't respond.)
It was all a lot simpler before you met her, wasn't it?

JESSICA

(Sits down) She's my only family.

PAT

(Hurt) I thought we were your family.

JESSICA

(Quickly) You are! You're my new family. It's just – *(careful)* Now, I have some old family, too.

PAT

(Brushes some sand off her clothes) I thought you wanted a new life. No ties from the past.

JESSICA

I did. But now I want a life that has room for Esther, too. Surely, I don't have to choose between a life in the Beaches and Esther. Surely, I can have both.

PAT

No, I don't think you can. Think about the baby. You don't want the baby growing up not knowing who he or she is.

JESSICA

The baby will know who she is. She'll be Protestant.

PAT

And how will she feel when other children ostracize her because of her Jewish aunt?
        (JESSICA is silent.)
Children can be cruel.

JESSICA

(Stands up) Shall we go for that walk? It feels cooler now.

Scene 3

> *(Late afternoon. The dining room. JESSICA is sitting at the table looking at one of the photographs. ESTHER enters with two glasses of iced tea.)*

ESTHER

How's that chair?

JESSICA

(Wiggles) A little wobbly.

ESTHER

Be careful. *(Sets the tea down on the table)* Here we are.

JESSICA

(Puts down the photograph and takes a glass) Thank you. I can't get over how young the three of you look in this picture. Where were you going?

ESTHER

(Sits down carefully and looks at the photograph) Let's see. I think we were going on a picnic. Speaking of picnics, I hear there was trouble in the Beaches over the long weekend. Were you there? It was so hot.

JESSICA

No. I decided to stay home and bury myself in a book. But the neighbours said the beach was packed. *(Uncomfortable)* They also said there were swastikas everywhere.
    (ESTHER shakes and tsks in disapproval.)
A few of the Jewish boys were so angry that they tore the swastika sweatshirts right off the backs of the boys who were wearing them. They called them Hitlerites.
    (ESTHER nods.)
(Hesitates) Esther, do you think they were Hitlerites?

ESTHER

What else would you call them?

JESSICA

Bradley says the Swastika Club isn't connected to any Nazi organizations.

ESTHER

Who's Bradley?

JESSICA

Larry's best friend.

ESTHER

And he wears a swastika on the beach?

JESSICA

(Embarrassed) Yes.

ESTHER

What does Larry say about all this?
   (JESSICA doesn't respond.)
He doesn't wear one too?
   (JESSICA doesn't respond.)
(Alarmed) Don't tell me that Larry is a member of that Club!

JESSICA

He thinks that by joining the Club, he'll be able to find a job.

ESTHER

He's not working?

JESSICA

No. He's been looking for a job for over a year.

ESTHER

So, you're paying for the house with what? The salary you get from the library?

JESSICA

(Nods) And our savings.

ESTHER

(Quiet) Your savings, *Mamaleh*? Or your father's?

JESSICA

What?

ESTHER

Shimon came to see me. I heard the whole story.

JESSICA

He came to see you? After all these years? Why?

ESTHER

He wants me to help him find you.

JESSICA

You didn't tell him where I was, did you?

ESTHER

No, no. I didn't say anything. Except …

JESSICA

Except what?

ESTHER

That I would help him find you.

JESSICA

Does he know that I work at the library?

ESTHER

No, no. I didn't say a word about the library.

JESSICA

I don't want to see him. He banished you from our home.

ESTHER

It's time to forgive.

JESSICA

What? After all those years we lost?

ESTHER

He's forgiven you.

JESSICA

(Tense laugh) He's forgiven me for what?

ESTHER

For taking his money.

JESSICA

I only took what belonged to me.

ESTHER

Do you know he lost the factory?

JESSICA

What? He had so many customers.

ESTHER

A lot can change in a year.

JESSICA

That's terrible.
        (ESTHER nods.)
(Pause) Do you think it might be my fault? *(Beat)* If I hadn't taken
the money … You think I should see him, don't you?

ESTHER

Forgiveness makes a family strong.
        (JESSICA doesn't respond.)
That's what your mother was telling you. *(Beat)* She's been very
busy lately, your mother. First you, then Shimon, then me. From you
and Shimon, she wants *s'lichah.* From me, she also wants *m'chilah.*

JESSICA

What's *m'chilah?*

ESTHER

M'chilah is also forgiveness. *S'lichah* is when you are ready to tell someone you forgive them or you are ready to ask for forgiveness. *M'chilah* is when you can say the past doesn't have to be different than it was. For me, it means letting go of all the bad feelings I have towards Shimon for all the years he wouldn't let me see you. But *kapparah* is even more difficult.

JESSICA

What's *kapparah*?

ESTHER

Kapparah is atonement. It's when you do something good for someone who needs to forgive you. It's a way of making something good come out of a bad situation. I promised Leah that I would be a mother to her daughter. That I would keep her daughter safe. With one ugly remark, I broke my promise to her. For all these years I've kept the guilt and anger of that broken promise inside of me. Leah says it's time to let that go, too. I have the chance to atone. *(Beat)* I want you to see your father. You need to ask him forgiveness for stealing his money and your mother's ring.

JESSICA

I didn't steal his money, I –

ESTHER

I understand that in a moment of anger, you felt that he owed it to you. But it wasn't yours to take, *Mamaleh*.

JESSICA

But I worked a whole year, for nothing. Don't you think –

ESTHER

It wasn't yours to take. Not the ring, not the money. *(Beat) S'lichach.*

JESSICA

I don't have the words.

ESTHER

Then you'll have to find them. And you'll have to make amends. You need to give him back the ring, and then you'll have to find a way to pay him back.

JESSICA

But we can't even make the payments on our house.

ESTHER

I didn't say it had to be today. But as soon as you can, you have to make amends. *Kapparah.* It's what your mother wants.

JESSICA

But it's not what I want. What does he have to give me? Nothing. Before I left, he wouldn't even talk to me.

ESTHER

It's not about what he has to give you. It's about what you share. It's about what we all share. We all lost Leah.

Scene 4

(Late afternoon. The porch, where BRADLEY and LARRY are reading The Evening Telegram.)

BRADLEY

(Puts down the paper) Jimmy's invited the boys in the Club to the ballgame at Christie Pits tomorrow night. I think we should go.

LARRY

(Puts down his paper) I thought the Mayor told the Club it had to disband.

BRADLEY

So what? That doesn't mean that we can't go out to a baseball game and support the team from St. Peter's.

LARRY
Who are they playing?

BRADLEY
The team from Harbord. The one with all the Jews.

LARRY
Why is Jimmy so interested in a game on the other side of town?

BRADLEY
One of the boys he works with at City Hall lives out by Christie Pits. He asked Jimmy to come out to the game. Just in case there's trouble. The fellow's name is Tom, and you'll be working with him, too, if you get that job Jimmy recommended you for. It will be a chance for you to meet him. *(Grins)* Besides, I think Jimmy's looking for a new house, and I want to be the one who sells it to him.

LARRY
How long do you think it will be before I hear about that job?

BRADLEY
Shouldn't be long now.

LARRY
I just got the first doctor's bill. We don't have enough money left to pay it.

BRADLEY
Is there anything you can sell?

LARRY
Not much.

BRADLEY
Doesn't Jessica have any jewelry?

LARRY

I'm not selling her wedding ring.

BRADLEY

Besides her wedding ring.

LARRY

There's a turquoise ring that belonged to her mother. *(Beat)* She hardly knew her.

BRADLEY

That should pay the doctor's bill.

Scene 5

(Afternoon. JESSICA and PAT are on the porch, knitting.)

PAT

So, have you thought of a name for the baby?

JESSICA

Leah. I wanted *Mama* to be remembered.

PAT

What if it is a boy?

JESSICA

Leonard. Lenny for short.

PAT

Larry's mother's name was Anne, and his father's name was Henry.

JESSICA

You don't like Leah and Leonard?

PAT

Well, they do sound very Jewish.

(PAT and JESSICA knit in silence.)

JESSICA

There's something I want to ask you. Last night, when I had to work late at the library, did Bradley and Larry go to the baseball game at Christie Pits?
(PAT doesn't answer.)
The secret to a good friendship is that good friends don't keep secrets.

PAT

Larry asked me not to say anything. He didn't want to upset you. Jimmy invited them. *(Quickly)* But Larry and Bradley weren't involved in the fighting. They left before the end of the game.

JESSICA

That fighting turned into a riot!
(PAT is silent.)
And did you hear what started it? Two boys brought out a swastika flag at the end of the game.

PAT

I'm going to make a matching set of leggings for this sweater. What colour would you prefer for the trim?

JESSICA

Pat, I'm afraid.

PAT

(Knits more quickly) There's nothing to be afraid of. Larry's going to get this job at City Hall, and you'll be able to leave the library and not have to travel downtown anymore. You'll give birth to a healthy, happy baby, who will be christened in church and become close

friends with Baby Emma. In a few years, the children will go to kindergarten, and we will cook and knit and read books together.

JESSICA
But –

(LARRY enters, wearing a big grin, and hurries up the porch steps.)

LARRY
I'm home!

(They stop knitting. LARRY climbs the stairs, walks over to JESSICA, kisses her on the forehead, sits down beside her and takes her hand.)

PAT
How did it go?

LARRY
(Grins) Jimmy was impressed. *(Beat)* He's going to hire me.

PAT
(Very excited) That's wonderful.

LARRY
(Also excited) I can't believe it. The City Hall job finally came through. We won't lose the house.

PAT
Bradley said that everything would work out. Congratulations!

LARRY
(Grins) Thanks. *(To JESSICA)* Now, we can buy that crib you saw at Eaton's.

JESSICA
(Smiles tensely) How closely will you have to work with Jimmy?

> LARRY

Very. *(Grins)* He's my boss.

> JESSICA

Then you can't take the job.

> LARRY

(Drops JESSICA's hand) What?

> JESSICA

I asked Pat if you and Bradley were at Christie Pits last night. She said Jimmy invited you to the game.
    (LARRY doesn't respond. PAT begins knitting again.)
I don't want you working for him.

> LARRY

Why?

> JESSICA

He's an anti-Semite.

> LARRY

(Stands up) Jess, your money's all gone. If I don't take that job, we'll have to sell the house.

> JESSICA

There are worse things.

> LARRY

(Starts pacing) Where would we live?

> JESSICA

I could talk to my Aunt Esther. She may have room for us in her house.

    (PAT stops knitting.)

118

LARRY

(Stops pacing) That woman who gave you the candlesticks? *(Incredulous)* Why would you want to go there? She lives downtown!

PAT

Maybe it's none of my business, but Bradley and I are your best friends. I can't listen to this and not say anything. What difference does it make that Jimmy doesn't care for Jews?

JESSICA

Because I still feel Jewish.

PAT

But that doesn't make any sense. You go to church with us on Sunday. You know all the words to the hymns. You can't still feel Jewish.

JESSICA

(Angry) Please don't tell me how I feel! I grew up Jewish. I lit candles on Friday night. And now, with all this trouble on the boardwalk and in the parks … It's ugly. And it frightens me. *(Resolute)* I want you to tell Jimmy you've changed your mind about the job.

LARRY

(Starts pacing again) There's something you don't know.

JESSICA

What?

LARRY

If I don't take Jimmy's job, we won't only lose the house. We'll lose the ring.

JESSICA

(Alarmed) Which ring?

LARRY
Your mother's turquoise ring. I had to sell it.

JESSICA
(Jumps out of her chair) What?

LARRY
(Miserable) I had no choice. The mortgage payment was due, and there wasn't enough money left to pay for that and the doctor's bill.

PAT
(Looks at JESSICA's right hand) But how – *(To JESSICA)* You never take it off.

JESSICA
My fingers started swelling up and the ring got too tight. I put it away in my jewelry box. For safekeeping.

LARRY
(Defensive) I didn't know what else to do.

JESSICA
(Ragged) It was one of the only memories I had of my mother.

PAT
(Puts down her knitting) I'm going inside to feed the baby.

(PAT goes inside the house.)

JESSICA
How could you?

LARRY
I did it to save our home. But now, we don't have to sell anything else. The new job starts next week and –

JESSICA

I told you. I don't want you working for Jimmy.

LARRY

But I have no other choice. I've been looking for a job for months, and there just isn't anything out there.

JESSICA

We can sell the house and move in with Esther.

LARRY

What? Ever since my dad died, there's only one thing I've ever really wanted. To live out his dream and raise a family in the Beaches. (Firm) I'm not going to sell the house. I'm going to take that job. (Quickly) Just for a little while. Until I can find something else.

JESSICA

(Also firm) I can't live here anymore.

LARRY

(Begins pacing) What do you mean you can't live here anymore? A year ago you couldn't wait to leave your father's house. You wanted to begin a new life. Well, this is our new life. We almost lost it. But we didn't. We can have it back. And now, you want to give it up?
> *(JESSICA walks back to the chair and sits down. LARRY leans against the porch.)*

JESSICA

When I was growing up, there weren't a lot of Jews in my neighbourhood. In elementary school, it didn't matter that I was Jewish. I was quiet and smart and was invited over to other girls' homes to play and do homework. But in high school, those girls dropped me, one by one.
> *(LARRY walks over to JESSICA and sits down beside her.)*

There was a small group of Jews at school. We stuck together. The one I liked the best was a boy named Lenny. He was brilliant. He wanted to go to university and become a lawyer and he had the marks to do it. *(Beat)* Lenny was fearless. He'd talk back. We told him that his smart remarks would get him in trouble. And they did. They beat him up so badly that he missed the last weeks of school. And then, he didn't go back. He went to work in a factory. Just like me. *(Beat)* When I told you I wanted to begin a new life, it was because my old life was so sad. So silent. So angry. So violent. I thought I could escape by marrying you and moving away. But the violence followed me. It followed me to Kew Beach and to the porch of my own home, where I found my husband wearing a swastika badge.

(LARRY looks at the ground.)

I can't escape it. I can only fight it. *(Beat)* I want to go home.

LARRY

What about what I want?

Scene 6

(Morning. ESTHER and JESSICA, at the dining room table.)

ESTHER

The room on the third floor is free. But it doesn't sound like he wants to come.

JESSICA

But if he does?

ESTHER

I have to be honest with you. I don't think much of a person who bullies Jews and sells what doesn't belong to him.

JESSICA

We were in a terrible situation. He made a mistake.

ESTHER

Two mistakes. Two very bad mistakes.

JESSICA

But you'll give him a second chance? *(Beat)* He's the father of my child.

ESTHER

(Hesitates, then) Well, if you can live with his mistakes, I guess I can too. If he decides to come, he's welcome. But I wouldn't count on it *Mamaleh.*

JESSICA

(Takes her hand and squeezes it) Thank you.

ESTHER

No need to thank me. We're family. *(Beat)* Make sure you don't forget the candlesticks.

Scene 7

BRADLEY

You can't turn your back on a good job at City Hall. Do you know how many people want this job? Hundreds!

LARRY

I know.

BRADLEY

Then why are we even having this conversation?

LARRY

Because if I take that job, I'll lose her. We're going to have a baby.

BRADLEY

A woman who really loves you wants what's best for you.

LARRY

Jessica loves me.

BRADLEY
Then why is she insisting you not take the job?

LARRY
I can't imagine selling the house and moving away.

BRADLEY
Of course not. This is where you belong.

LARRY
But Jessica says she can't live here.

BRADLEY
Because she's never belonged here.

LARRY
That's not true. She loved it here. She loved our house. She loved
Baby Emma –

BRADLEY
She may have liked it here, but she never belonged here. *(Beat)* You
should have told me. Why didn't you tell me?

LARRY
Because I wanted you to like her. I wanted you to get to know her,
and see what a wonderful girl she is –

BRADLEY
There were lots of wonderful girls. Why her?

LARRY
She had the saddest eyes.

BRADLEY
You won't get this opportunity again.

LARRY

I know.

Scene 8

(Twilight. The dining room. JESSICA is working on an account ledger at the dining room table. SHIMON enters and stands at the dining room entrance.)

SHIMON

Jessica?

(JESSICA looks up. There are a few seconds of silence).

JESSICA

Hello, *Papa.*

(JESSICA stands up.)

SHIMON

Esther said you're expecting me.
(JESSICA doesn't respond.)
Can I sit down?
(SHIMON begins to sit down.)

JESSICA

Be careful. The leg's –

SHIMON

Broken.
(SHIMON and JESSICA both sit down, carefully. SHIMON takes out a handkerchief and wipes his forehead)
The beginning of September, but still so hot.
(JESSICA doesn't respond).
Esther says you're starting up your own bookkeeping business.

                        JESSICA

Yes.

                        SHIMON

You think you can make a living?

                        JESSICA

The business will grow. And I have a job at the children's library. At
least, for a little while.

                        SHIMON

So you're planning to stay in the neighbourhood?

                        JESSICA

Yes.

                        SHIMON

With your husband?

                        JESSICA

I don't know. *(Changing the topic)* Esther said you wanted to talk to
me.

                        SHIMON

How could you leave just like that? And take your *Mama's* ring?

        (JESSICA is silent.)

Your mother loved that ring. She said turquoise was magic. It could
help a man and his wife in bad times.

        (SHIMON looks at JESSICA's hand.)

You aren't wearing it.

                        JESSICA

My first child hasn't been born yet. *(Beat)* I left because I was angry.

                        SHIMON

(Stands up) And what were you so angry about?

126

JESSICA

(Also stands up) I was eighteen years old, doing your books, but *you* decided whom I could or couldn't see. Whom I could talk to, whom I couldn't. I was a prisoner in my own home.

SHIMON

The world is a dangerous place. I was only trying to protect you.

JESSICA

You don't need to protect a grown daughter.

SHIMON

Your mother was older than you are now when she first became sick. I didn't notice how sick she was until it was too late to help her.

JESSICA

You tried to separate Larry and me.

SHIMON

And where is he now, this wonderful husband of yours?

JESSICA

If you had accepted him from the beginning, Larry wouldn't have lost his job. We wouldn't have run away. Who knows what would have happened?

SHIMON

He lost his job?

JESSICA

Of course he lost his job. After you called his boss.

SHIMON

I just wanted him out of the factory. Put on another delivery route.

JESSICA

Well, he lost his job.

SHIMON

Why didn't you tell me?

JESSICA

Don't you remember? You stopped talking to me. *(Sharp)* Just like you stopped talking to Esther.
> *(SHIMON steps back, as if unexpectedly hit.)*

(Accusing) I had an aunt I never knew. I was a little girl without a mother, and you took my aunt away from me.

SHIMON

(Voice rises in anger) I have made peace with Esther.

JESSICA

(Quiet) Please don't yell at me.

SHIMON

(Struggles to lower his voice) Now, I want make peace with you. Soon, it will be Yom Kippur.

JESSICA

Since when are you so religious? If it's so important to make peace at Yom Kippur, why did you turn Esther away all those years? It's not always so easy to make peace, is it? I'm not interested.

SHIMON

(Hurt) I should go. *(Beat)* Could I see the ring?

JESSICA

Why?

SHIMON

It reminds me of Leah.

JESSICA

Did you love her?

SHIMON

Of course I loved her. *(Places his hand on top of the chair)* She was smart. She helped me in the business. Before you were born, she kept the books. Just like you did. She always knew what was what. It was a comfort.

JESSICA

(Sits down carefully) So, she gave you comfort. And what did you give to her?

SHIMON

(Also sits down carefully) She had a nice home. We had a child together. The day you were born was the happiest day of her life.

JESSICA

What was it like when she got sick?

SHIMON

Terrible. We went to see a lot of doctors. There was nothing that anyone could do.

JESSICA

Nothing?

SHIMON

Nothing.

JESSICA

So you took her to the hospital?

SHIMON

No. She wanted to die at home, so she could see you every day she had left.

JESSICA

(Tearful) So who took care of her? Esther?

SHIMON

No. I did.

JESSICA

What about work?

SHIMON

I stayed home from work.

JESSICA

You stayed home from work?

SHIMON

There was a lot to do. Two, three times a day, I gave her a bath. Changed her clothes, changed her sheets. Leah hated not being clean. *(Sighs)* Every day, Esther came to the house after work, and we would try to get her to eat something. But she was never hungry. At night, we turned off the lights. They hurt her eyes. We lit candles, and Esther would bring you in to say good night.

JESSICA

(Tearful) Tell me about the night she died.

SHIMON

The night she died, she thanked me. I didn't know she was sick until it was too late to help her, but she thanked me for taking care of her when she was dying. It was never hard to please Leah.

JESSICA

There is something I have to tell you.

SHIMON

What is it?

JESSICA

You'll be angry.

SHIMON

(Leans forward) Tell me.

JESSICA

Mama's ring is gone.

SHIMON

Gone? How is it gone? It was lost?

JESSICA

(Takes a deep breath) Sold. Larry had to sell it.

SHIMON

(Stands up, his voice rises in anger) He sold Leah's ring?

JESSICA

(Stands up, quiet) To save our house.

SHIMON

(Raises his voice, enraged) How dare he? How dare *you*?

JESSICA

(Raises her voice) Please don't yell at me. I didn't know he was going to sell the ring.

(SHIMON's shoulders begin to shake with anger and sorrow.)

SHIMON

(Shakes his head) What a shame. What a shame. What a shame. *(Beat)* You were right to leave him.

JESSICA

I didn't want to leave him. *(With pain)* I wanted him to come with me to Esther's. *(Beat)* I still hope he will.

SHIMON

(Shakes his head) How can you live with such a man?

JESSICA

He made a mistake. People make mistakes.

SHIMON

But to sell your mother's ring!

(JESSICA begins to sway, and clutches onto the table.)

SHIMON

What's wrong? Are you feeling sick?

JESSICA

A little lightheaded.

SHIMON

Is there something I can do?

JESSICA

Call Esther. *(Anxious)* Something's not right.

Scene 9

(Night. BRADLEY is sitting on the porch. LARRY enters, and slowly walks up to the porch).

BRADLEY

(Calls out) How is she?

LARRY

She's sleeping.
(LARRY slowly makes his way up the stairs of the porch and sits down in the nearest chair.)
(Anguished) We lost the baby.

BRADLEY

What happened?

LARRY

(Distraught) The doctor's not sure. But he did say her blood pressure was much too high.

BRADLEY

How long will she be in the hospital?

LARRY

I don't know. A few days.

BRADLEY

You know, maybe it's for the best.

LARRY

(Incredulous) What?

BRADLEY

It wasn't meant to be. *(Beat)* Now, you can move on.

LARRY

(Anger rising) What are you saying?

BRADLEY

There's no baby to hold you back.

LARRY

(Stands up, shouts) Shut up! Just shut up. I wanted this baby. I wanted to be a father.
   (Starts pacing)

BRADLEY

(Remains seated, calm) Of course you did, but you couldn't have raised a half-Jew baby in Balmy Beach.

LARRY

(Stops pacing) What?

BRADLEY

(Stands up) You heard me.

LARRY

(Furious, kicks the fence) I can raise my children anywhere I want.

BRADLEY

(Superior) Don't be so innocent. Jessica isn't. She understands. We don't want Jews here. That's why she left. Now that she's gone back to where she belongs, you, my friend, have been given a second chance.

LARRY

(Approaches Bradley) What?

BRADLEY

Give it some time. There are lots of other wonderful girls to have babies with.

> *(LARRY punches BRADLEY in the stomach. Surprised, BRADLEY doubles over and falls to his knees. Equally surprised, LARRY falls to his knees beside BRADLEY.)*

LARRY

(In tears) I hate you right now. My baby's dead. I really hate you.

Scene 10

> *(Early evening. The dining room. LARRY is standing at the entrance of the room carrying* Jane Eyre. *Esther is setting the table for dinner.)*

LARRY

I found it. It was on the bookshelf. *(Checks his watch)* Visiting hours will be over soon. I should get going.

ESTHER

Have you eaten anything?

LARRY

I'll eat when I get home. I don't want to keep her waiting.

ESTHER

(Reaching into the bowl of fruit on the table and handing him an apple) Here, have a piece of fruit, at least.

LARRY

(Puts the apple in his pocket) Thanks. *(Begins to exit)* See you later.

ESTHER

Wait a minute. *(Beat)* How are *you*?

LARRY

What do you mean?

ESTHER

You look a little tired.

LARRY

(Smiles to reassure her) I'm fine.

ESTHER

You lost a baby, too.

LARRY

(Suddenly tearful) It hurts. I feel like I have a big hole in my heart.

ESTHER

(Walks over and gives him a hug) I know. *(Beat)* Come, sit down. Just for a minute.
        (LARRY begins to sit down.)
Be careful. The leg is loose.
        (LARRY kneels down and takes a look at the chair leg.)

135

                    LARRY

I could fix this for you.

                    ESTHER

You think so?

                    LARRY

Sure.

                    ESTHER

The other one's like that too.

                    LARRY

I can fix both of them. I'll come over after the hospital later this
week.

                    ESTHER

Wonderful. And I'll make you some dinner.

                    LARRY

You don't have to go to any trouble.

                    ESTHER

No trouble. Come, sit down a minute. Just be careful.
        (Both sit down carefully.)
You were excited about having this baby.

                    LARRY

I couldn't wait to be a father. I wanted to do all the things my father
did with me. And all the things he didn't.

                    ESTHER

He must have been a young man when he died.

                    LARRY

It was all so unexpected.

ESTHER

Like losing the baby.

LARRY

I never said goodbye.
(ESTHER takes his hand in hers.)
I've been trying to keep him alive. In that house we bought in the Beaches, my father is alive.

Scene 11

(Late afternoon. The porch where LARRY is putting some of JESSICA's books in a bag. SHIMON enters and approaches the porch.)

SHIMON

(Tentative) Hello?

LARRY

(Surprised, jumps up) What's wrong? Is Jessica all right?

SHIMON

Nothing's wrong. Jessica's fine. *(Beat)* Well, not fine. But better. She's glad to be back at Esther's.

LARRY

That's good.

SHIMON

Do you mind if I sit down?

LARRY

No. Come on up.

SHIMON

Esther says you visited Jessica every day after work. You read to her to keep her mind off the baby.

(LARRY nods.)

SHIMON

I read to Leah, too. *(Sad)* Before she was too sick to listen. *(Beat)* So. Are you still working at City Hall?

LARRY

Why are you interested?

SHIMON

You're my daughter's husband.

LARRY

(Surprised, pauses) Actually, I'm looking for another job.

SHIMON

I see. Any success?

LARRY

Not yet.

SHIMON

You need to start your own business.

LARRY

What?

SHIMON

Like Jessica. You could learn bookkeeping, too.

LARRY

(Surprised) Me?

SHIMON

I taught Jessica how to do the books, why not you?

LARRY

Why would you do this for me? You're the one who got me fired.

SHIMON

I didn't – I'm trying to make it up to you.

LARRY

And you think I'd make a good bookkeeper?

SHIMON

To be honest, I don't know. A man who sells his wife's ring without asking her doesn't make a good bookkeeper. *(Beat)* But you're not the first person in the world to make a big mistake. My daughter tells me that she still loves you. And I can see that you are a devoted husband. So, I came to see if you will come to live at Esther's. If you come, I'll teach you how to do the books.
　　(LARRY doesn't respond.)
Look, you'll be doing me a favour.

LARRY

A favour?

SHIMON

Esther says I must atone. I'm not a religious man. But Jessica is still angry with me. If you agree to live at Esther's, then maybe she will forgive me and we can finally have peace in the family.
　　(LARRY doesn't respond.)
So, what do you think?

LARRY

I'm not sure she'll take me back.

SHIMON

You won't know unless you ask.

LARRY

Is there room for me in Esther's house?

                         SHIMON
There's a room for everyone in Esther's house. Not a quiet room,
mind you, but a room.

                          LARRY
I don't need quiet.

Scene 12

          *(Sunset. The dining room. JESSICA is working at the table.
          ESTHER enters, followed by LARRY. They both stand at the
          entrance of the dining room.)*

                         ESTHER
Am I disturbing you?

                         JESSICA
(Head down, concentrating) I'm just finishing up here.

                         ESTHER
You have some guests.

                         JESSICA
(Head still down) Who?

                          LARRY
Me.

                         JESSICA
(Looks up surprised) Oh!

          *(JESSICA stands up quickly, winces, places her hand on her
          lower back for support and smoothes her skirt.)*

                         ESTHER
Your father's here too.

JESSICA

My father?

ESTHER

He can wait. I'll go make some tea.

(ESTHER exits.)

LARRY

How are you feeling?

JESSICA

(Puts one hand on the back of her chair and rubs her lower back with the other) Better.

LARRY

That's good. *(Pauses, takes a risk)* I miss you, Jess.

JESSICA

I miss you, too.

LARRY

I came to talk about getting back together.

JESSICA

I'm not going back to the Beach. This is my home now.

LARRY

I understand. *(Beat)* I was thinking that I could move in with you and Esther and help you in the business. Your father says he'll teach me how to do the books.

JESSICA

(Very surprised) When did you talk to my father?

LARRY

He came to see me.

141

JESSICA
My father took the streetcar to Kew Beach to see you and said he'd –

LARRY
Teach me bookkeeping. You know, I always liked math.

JESSICA
Why?

LARRY
Why did I like math?

JESSICA
No. Why does he want to teach you bookkeeping?

LARRY
So I can earn a decent living. And make enough to raise a family.

JESSICA
(Straightens the ledgers on the table) What about the job at City Hall?

LARRY
I left City Hall. You were right. People there don't like Jews. There was a lot of nasty talk. *(Beat)* Jessica, I want to apologize for the swastika. I was wrong to wear it. I hated parading down the boardwalk. But I was so desperate to get a job that – I made a mistake. I won't ever wear it again. Can you forgive me?

JESSICA
(Doesn't respond, then) What's happened to the house?

LARRY
I sold it.

JESSICA

(Very surprised) Sold it?

LARRY

Before quitting. So we wouldn't lose it to the bank.

JESSICA

You chose that house over me.

LARRY

Living there was never the same after you left. And after losing the baby *(falters)* ... I can't lose you too.

JESSICA

It was your father's dream to live in the Beach.

LARRY

I know. I've been spending a lot of time down by lake thinking. I need to find my own dream. One that keeps me close to him, but close to you, too. My father always wanted to own his own business. I think he'd approve. *(Moving closer to JESSICA, softly)* I love you, Jessica. I want to spend the rest of my life with you. Have children together. Please, let's try again.

JESSICA

It will be a very long time before we'll own our own home. I pay Esther room and board, and I'm planning to pay my father back the money I took from him. The business will grow, but it will take us years to save up for a home.

LARRY

I know.

JESSICA

Bradley won't visit you here. And I won't visit him and Pat there.

LARRY

I understand.

JESSICA

But he's been like a brother to you.

LARRY

It's true. But it's … *(hesitates)* It's time to move on. For now, at least.

JESSICA

Are you sure?

LARRY

Yes, I'm sure.

JESSICA

(Reaches over and takes his hand) All right, we can try again.

LARRY

You want to try again?

JESSICA

Yes. Like Jane Eyre and Rochester.
> *(LARRY gently pulls her to him and gives JESSICA a short tentative kiss that is full of yearning. ESTHER and SHIMON enter and stand at the entrance of the room. ESTHER is carrying a* yahrtzeit *candle. JESSICA breaks away from the embrace.)*

Esther told me that we're both welcome here.

ESTHER

That's right, I did.

SHIMON

(To LARRY) So? She's taking you back?

LARRY

Yes. *(Smiles)* There's room for me at Esther's.

SHIMON

(To LARRY) What did I tell you?

JESSICA

(Pauses. To SHIMON) I have something for you. *(Takes an envelope off the dining room table and hands it to him)* It's a first payment. Of the money I took. It won't bring back the factory, but at least I can try to make amends.
    (SHIMON is silent.)
You won't accept my apology?

ESTHER

Of course, he will.

SHIMON

Esther, I can speak for myself.

ESTHER

So speak!

SHIMON

What's done is done.

  (SHIMON sighs gently and looks at his watch.)

JESSICA

Is there somewhere you need to be?

SHIMON

Esther and I are going to *shul*.

JESSICA

Shul? We never went to *shul*.

                              SHIMON

It's the anniversary of your mother's death. We're going to light a candle for Leah's *yahrtzeit* and then we're going to shul to say *kaddish* for Leah – may she rest in peace.

                              ESTHER

(Whispers to Shimon) Invite them.

                              SHIMON

Maybe you'd like to come with us?

                              JESSICA

(Quiet) Kaddish. We could say *kaddish.*

                              SHIMON

Yes. For your mother.

                              JESSICA

And for the baby. Larry, come to *shul* with me. We'll mourn for *Mama* and we'll mourn for the baby.

                              LARRY

All right. I'll get my coat.

          (LARRY, JESSICA and SHIMON exit. ESTHER lights the yahrtzeit *candle on the dining room table, watches the flame burn, then exits. Lights slowly fade on the dining room.)*

End of play

ANA'S SHADOW

DEVELOPMENT HISTORY

Early drafts of *Ana's Shadow* were read and critiqued by Clare Alcott, Irena Kohn, Joanne Latimer, and Jocelyn Wickett.

A five-day workshop exploring the characters, themes and politics of *Ana's Shadow* was conducted by Gailey Road Productions from August 22-26, 2011. The workshop was facilitated by Jocelyn Wickett, managed by Gillian Lewis, and archived by Amy Gullage. A public reading of the play was undertaken at the 519 Church Street Community Centre on August 26, 2011. Collaborating artists who participated in the workshop and reading were:

Rebecca Applebaum
Julie Burris
Hannah Dean (songwriter and musician)
Esteé Feldman
Joanne Latimer
Jorie Morrow
Chantelle Pike (songwriter and musician)
Supinder Wraich

Ana's Shadow was published by *Canadian Theatre Review,* Issue *151,* in July 2012.

A digital recording of a rehearsed reading of the play, featuring the cast listed above, was produced in May 2013, and is available for download from www.gaileyroad.com

This play is dedicated to the late Rosalind Zinman and to the late Sharon Rosenberg.

CHARACTERS

HARRIET: Mother of three daughters, the first two adopted from Colombia. Jewish. Age 49. Undergoing treatment for breast cancer.

LUISA: Harriet's eldest daughter, adopted from Colombia at the age of 10. Age 22. Preparing to study medicine at university, raising money to build a medical clinic in Bogotá.

ANA: Harriet's middle daughter, adopted from Colombia at the age of 7. Age 19. Dropped out of her first year of university to take care of Harriet.

CLARE: Harriet's youngest daughter, not adopted. Age 16. Attending high school, raising money to build a medical clinic in Bogotá.

MARTY: Harriet's wife. Age 44.

ANITA: Founder of Global Family, an international adoption agency. A family friend. Jewish. Age 55.

SETTING

Harriet's kitchen, Toronto, Canada.
The recent present

***

Prelude

(HARRIET's kitchen. ANA is composing a new song. She has a lovely singing voice, and it's clear she loves to sing.)

Scene 1 Passover

(HARRIET's kitchen. April. There are two closed cardboard boxes containing childrens' books in clear view on stage. The family is sitting at the kitchen table, celebrating Passover with a Seder.)

CLARE

(Reading from the Haggadah *ANA put together)* And now, our telling of the Passover story is over. Next year, may we celebrate Passover in a world at peace. May Israel and her neighbours take courageous new steps to bring new cooperation and peace to the Middle East. And next year, may we celebrate Passover with Harriet in good health and fully recovered.

(ANA grabs HARRIET's hand. HARRIET gives it a squeeze and then takes CLARE's hand.)

HARRIET

Thank you.

CLARE

L'shana haba-a biy'rushalayim! Next year in Jerusalem!

LUISA

Very nice.

HARRIET

(With pleasure) A lovely Seder. Really lovely.

ANA

(Starts passing around matzo *and* charoset, *which is already on the table)* Seder lite. I hope it was okay. I wasn't sure how tired you'd be.

HARRIET

It was perfect. I'm actually feeling pretty good tonight.

MARTY

Thanks so much for putting it all together.

ANA

Everyone helped.

MARTY

Yeah, but you did most of the cooking.

ANA

I don't mind. I love Passover.

HARRIET

Me too. I'm celebrating Passover just like I did last year, and just like I will be next year.

ANA

Should I bring out the soup?

HARRIET

In a minute. *(To Luisa)* What happened to Jorge?

LUISA

I changed my mind.

HARRIET

Why? I wanted to meet him.

CLARE

I met him!

HARRIET

I wanted to meet him too.

LUISA

You'll meet him. Marty, Ana and I decided tonight should be just for us.

150

CLARE

He's very cute. And he wants to go to med school just like Luisa so he can join Doctors without Borders. *(To Luisa) Verdad* [Right]*?*

LUISA

Es verdad [Right].

MARTY

Very impressive.

CLARE

And guess where he's from? Bogotá!

HARRIET

(Smiles) And what's he doing this summer?

CLARE

Coming with us to help build the clinic and go see his *familia*.

HARRIET

What? How come I haven't heard about this before?

LUISA

It's no big deal. He's going to visit family. And while he's there, he'll help out once in a while.

HARRIET

But you and Clare are going to stay at the orphanage with the Sisters, like you planned?

LUISA

Yes, of course.

HARRIET

And Jorge is going to stay where?

LUISA

With his family.

HARRIET

I want to meet him before you go, okay?

ANA

He's like four years older than Luisa.

HARRIET

What?

CLARE

Not four, three. Just three.

ANA

Okay, three. That's still old.

LUISA

No, it's not.

ANA

Yes, it is.

CLARE

(Changes subject) I wish you and Marty were going with us.

HARRIET

Me too.

MARTY

Next summer. We'll go next summer.

LUISA

(To Ana) It's not too late for *you* to change your mind about coming.

ANA

Not interested.

LUISA

So, what are you going to do all summer?

MARTY

(To LUISA) You promised.

ANA

What I'm doing now. Going to chemo with Harriet. Cooking for Harriet.

LUISA

You need to be doing something *besides* helping Harriet.

HARRIET

She's writing songs.

LUISA

Besides writing songs. She needs to get out.

ANA

I get out.

LUISA

(Lightly) Going to Loblaw's and the health food store isn't getting out. When's the last time you saw any of your friends? Like Helen?

ANA

Since when are you so interested in my friends?

LUISA

When's the last time you saw Helen?

ANA

She's busy. With school.

LUISA

(Lightly) Like you should be.

MARTY

Okay, that's –

ANA

She's practicing.

LUISA

Practicing for what?

CLARE

Canadian Idol.

LUISA

(Rolls her eyes) Canadian Idol. She's wasting her time. The only people who actually vote on that show are 11-year-old girls and their mothers. And they always vote for the boys. *(Beat)* Come to Bogotá with me and Clare.

ANA

How many times do I have to tell you? I don't *want* to go Bogotá this summer. I'm staying here and helping Harriet.

LUISA

But Marty will be off.

ANA

So?

LUISA

How long are you going to keep this up?

MARTY

Luisa, please.

HARRIET

The chemo will be over by the end of summer, and she'll go back to university in the fall, just like she promised. Right?

ANA

(Unenthusiastic) Yeah.

LUISA

Don't you want a chance to find out more about your heritage?

ANA

Who do you think planned this whole Seder?

LUISA

Not this heritage. Your Colombian heritage. Your genetic heritage. You need to go back to where you came from to really know who you are. Who you want to be. *(Beat)* I found a cheap ticket for you.

ANA

(Upset) What?

LUISA

But we have to pay for it by the middle of the week.

ANA

(More upset) I told you. I'm not going anywhere until Harriet's okay. Why would you buy me a ticket?

MARTY

(To LUISA) Really *(as in 'why would you buy her a ticket knowing how she feels about going back to Bogotá?').*

LUISA

I didn't buy it. I reserved it.

ANA

155

Well I don't want it. No matter how many times you keep asking me, I'm not going with you.

LUISA

But it's such a good opportunity to –

ANA

(Very upset) Stop pushing me. Just leave me alone! Why can't you just let it go! If I ever want to go to Bogotá, you'll be the first to know.

MARTY

(Stands up) Okay. That's clear. *(To Luisa)* Help me clear the table so Ana can bring out the soup. It's Passover.

LUISA

(Stands up, picks up some plates) You're missing out on a great opportunity.

ANA

(Stands up, picks up some plates) No, I'm not.

MARTY

(Begs) Luisa.

LUISA

I'm sorry. But she's stuck. And maybe if –

ANA

(Angry) I am not stuck.

LUISA

You dropped out of school.

ANA

I didn't drop out. I'm going back. I hate you when you're like this. Stop it. Just stop it.

(ANA leaves the kitchen.)

HARRIET
(Stands up, puts her hand on Luisa's arm) That's enough.

LUISA
(Takes a second, then) Okay. I'm sorry. *(To MARTY)* I'll clear. You sit.

(Music is played to transition from Scene 1 to 2.)

Scene 2 Birth Family

(Harriet's kitchen. April. Clare is wiping off, dusting and packing away the Passover haggadot *into a plastic container for storage.)*

CLARE
Why does Luisa think that Ana needs to find out about her genetic heritage?

HARRIET
So she knows what she might have inherited from her biological mother and father.

CLARE
Maybe she looks like her birth mother.

HARRIET
Maybe.

CLARE
Maybe she gets her voice from her.

HARRIET
Maybe. *(Beat)* Has Luisa told you she wants to find out more about her birth family when you're in Bogotá this summer?

CLARE

(Uncomfortable) Maybe.

HARRIET

It's okay to tell me. It's good for your sisters to find out as much as they can about their birth family.

CLARE

You think?

HARRIET

Yes.

CLARE

But don't you think they've inherited things from our family too?

HARRIET

(Gives CLARE a hug) Of course. Living with us has given them lots of things. We've loved them. Supported them to do the things they cared about.

CLARE

Like fundraising for the clinic.

HARRIET

Yeah. *(Points to one of the* haggadot*)* The cover on that one is torn. You need to tape it before you put it away.

CLARE

(Puts it aside) Okay. Do you think that she'll find anyone from her birth family?

HARRIET

She might. But it could take a while.

CLARE

We're going to be there for two months.

HARRIET

Two months isn't a very long time. But maybe the Sisters at the orphanage have records that will help.

CLARE

I hope so.

HARRIET

Me too.

CLARE

Mum …

HARRIET

What?

CLARE

It's okay, right?

HARRIET

Is what okay?

CLARE

That I'm going to Bogotá with Luisa?

HARRIET

Of course, it's okay.

CLARE

(Anxious) You don't want me to stay home and help you?

HARRIET

No. Marty will be finished teaching by the time you leave.

CLARE

(Reluctant) If Ana changes her mind and wants to go with Luisa, I could stay home.

HARRIET

That's very generous of you. But I don't think Ana will change her mind. And even if she did. All three of you can go. I'll be fine.

CLARE

(Relieved) Are you sure?

HARRIET

I'm sure. You and Luisa have been fundraising for the clinic and planning this trip for three years. I want you to go. It's important. Just because I'm having a lousy summer doesn't mean you have to. But I want to meet Jorge before you go. Okay?

CLARE

Okay.

(Music is played to transition from Scene 2 to 3.)

Scene 3 Alone Time

(HARRIET's kitchen. April. MARTY is unpacking supplies from the pharmacy and the health food store. HARRIET is drinking tea, watching her.)

MARTY

(Very pleased) Look what I found.

HARRIET

What?

MARTY

The skin oil you like so much. We ran out, and I've been having trouble finding it. But today … *(Holds up a small bottle of oil)*.

HARRIET

(Muted) That's great. Thanks.

MARTY

You've been complain– saying that your skin's really flaky again. I thought I could rub in some oil. *(Beat)* Maybe put on some jazz. Light a candle. The girls are all out.

HARRIET

I think I need a nap this afternoon.

MARTY

Sure. Okay. Maybe after the nap.

HARRIET

We'll see.

MARTY

Sure. If you're not up for it, we could just put on a movie. Have some popcorn. *(Rummages through one of her bags) Thelma and Louise.* On sale.

HARRIET

(Manages a smile) Maybe. We'll see.

MARTY

It's been a while since we've had any alone time.

HARRIET

I know. I'm just so damn tired today.

MARTY

Okay. Let's get you to bed.

HARRIET

It's okay. I can get there myself.

(She gets up off the chair slowly, with effort.)

MARTY

You sure?

HARRIET

I'm sure.
> *(Fatigued, she walks very slowly, step by step, in a shuffle.)*

MARTY

(Doesn't follow) Okay. *(Beat)* What if I lie down with you?

HARRIET

(Continues walking, unenthusiastic) If you want to. *(Beat)* I feel like I weigh a ton.

MARTY

(Speaking to her back) I know.

HARRIET

(Irritated) No, you don't.

MARTY

(Careful) Can I bring you something? Water? More tea?

HARRIET

(Still irritated) Uh-uh.

MARTY

You're sure?

HARRIET

(Still irritated) Uh-huh.

MARTY

(Apologetic) I'm mothering too much.

HARRIET

(Still irritated) Uh-huh.

MARTY

(Frustrated) I'm sorry. It's just … Sometimes … It's just that I want so badly to help you, and nothing I do seems right.

HARRIET

(Stops walking, turns to face her) I know.

MARTY

(Angry) No, you don't.

> *(The room is tense.)*

HARRIET

Come here.
> *(MARTY walks over. HARRIET takes her hand and breaks the tension. As HARRIET takes MARTY's hand, MARTY's relief is visible.)*

I've been thinking. I've decided that who you vomit with is more important than who you have sex with.

MARTY

(Laughs) Then I must be very important.

HARRIET

Very.
> *(She begins walking/shuffling again, still holding MARTY's hand. MARTY walks with her)*

I've decided something else.

MARTY

What?

HARRIET

I want to buy a really good audio system. Something expensive that Ana can use to record her songs.

> *(Music is played to transition from Scene 3 to 4.)*

Scene 4 Cancer

(HARRIET's kitchen. April. ANA is consulting a vegan cookbook and making a list of the food she and MARTY need to shop for. MARTY is reading the newspaper while she waits for ANA to finish the list.)

ANA

(Adds one or two things to the list). Okay. That's everything, I think.

MARTY

(Reading her paper, half listening) Yeah?

ANA

A lot of people are becoming vegan, you know. Most of them just think a vegan lifestyle is a better way to live. But some of them are dealing with cancer. Just like us.

MARTY

(Stops reading) Yeah?

ANA

They think eating vegan may prevent their cancer from coming back.

MARTY

It's a hard diet to follow.

ANA

Yeah, but I'm moving slowly. Integrating it into our diets a little bit at a time.

MARTY

Just make sure that we're eating enough protein.

ANA

Don't worry. I've got it under control. *(Puts the list in her pocket)* You ready to go?

MARTY

Yeah. *(Beat)* There's just one thing. Before we go.

ANA

What?

MARTY

School.

ANA

(Tenses) What about it?

MARTY

What happened?

ANA

Didn't Harriet tell you?

MARTY

She told me. But I don't get it. I didn't see it coming.
(ANA doesn't respond. She takes the list of out her pocket and
starts looking at it again)
You didn't just wake up one day and say "I'm not going to school
anymore".

ANA

(Still looking at the list) No.

MARTY

So, when did it start?

ANA

(Still looking at the list) What?

MARTY

Feeling like you wanted to leave.

ANA

I don't know. The first week back. *(Looks up)* It was hard. Everyone else was excited to be back. And I wasn't. I wasn't into it at all. I wanted to be home with Harriet. My first class was at ten. But sometimes Harriet didn't get up 'till ten. And I wanted to spend some time with her before I left for school. Especially during the first week after chemo, when she felt so awful. But I couldn't. So I'd sit there, wondering how she was doing, how her morning was going instead of listening to what was going on in class. When it came time to write the first quiz, I was too far behind. So I dropped the ten o'clock class. And then, Harriet and I got into a morning routine. And I loved being home with Harriet in the morning. So, I dropped the one o'clock class. Then Harriet agreed to try going vegan. It takes time to shop for the right food. To learn how to eat vegan. So, I decided to drop the rest of the courses and defer for a year. I talked to someone. I did it properly. I can go back. I promised Harriet I'd go back.

MARTY

Maybe you could transfer into another program. Like nutrition.

ANA

You need to have a lot of science courses to get into a program like that.

MARTY

You could upgrade.

ANA

If I were into it.

MARTY

You're not into it.

ANA

I'm only going vegan to help us deal with the cancer. Let's go.

MARTY

So, it's about the cancer.

ANA

Everything's about the cancer.

MARTY

Yeah.

ANA

Let's go.

MARTY

In a minute. What does it feel like to you?

ANA

What?

MARTY

Dealing with the cancer.

ANA

I don't know. Like I'm living under a big shadow.

MARTY

Right.

ANA

What does it feel like to you?

MARTY

The same. But I'm trying to see it differently. Like I'm living *beside* the shadow. Not under it.

ANA

What's the difference?

                    MARTY

When I'm beside the shadow, I can still see it. I know it's there. I can
keep my eye on it, but it doesn't always stay the same size.
Sometimes it's taller, sometimes it's shorter. And when it's smaller, I
can be a little less anxious, a little less scared about what's going to
happen. When I live beside the cancer, I don't carry it on my
shoulders. Or around my neck. It's still there, beside me. But it's not
strangling me.

                    ANA

It's strangling me.

                    MARTY

(Picks up the car keys off the table) Yeah. But not always. Not when
you're singing.

                    ANA

No. Not when I'm singing.

                    MARTY

Harriet loves listening to you sing. It's how she lives beside the
shadow.

          *(Music is played to transition from Scene 4 to 5. HARRIET
          brings out a cardboard box and three children's books. She
          puts the box on top of the other boxes and puts in the books.)*

Scene 5 Competition

          *(HARRIET's kitchen. May. There are now three boxes of
          children's books on stage. HARRIET, MARTY and all three
          girls are going through a pile of ANA and LUISA's clothes
          trying to pick out the outfits ANA should wear to compete on
          Canadian Idol.)*

                    MARTY

Okay. Jeans. You definitely need jeans. Two pairs? Three?

ANA

Two.

LUISA

What about a skirt? *(Holds up a skirt she bought in Colombia)* I can lend you a skirt.

ANA

No. No skirts. Just jeans. And maybe one other pair of pants.

MARTY

And sneakers. Two? Three?

ANA

It depends on what tops I take.

LUISA

(Holds up some tops she bought in Colombia) Here. These are from Bogotá. Try them on.

ANA

They won't fit.

LUISA

How do you know? Try them on.

ANA

I'm not going for that kind of look.

CLARE

I can't believe you're auditioning for *Canadian Idol.* How did it happen?

ANA

Not now. I'm trying to pack.

CLARE

You said you'd tell me while you packed. All my friends are waiting.

ANA

It's too late now.

CLARE

But I need to know. I promised I'd tell them as soon as I found out.

ANA

(To MARTY) Can you tell her? I need to look for more tops.

MARTY

Yeah, okay.

LUISA

Do you want some help?

ANA

No.

(ANA exits)

CLARE

So, tell me.

MARTY

Okay. Ana is standing in line with Helen while she waits for her turn to audition. And there's a girl standing behind them. What's her name again?

LUISA

Don't ask me. I wasn't there.

MARTY

Lidia. Her name was Lidia. And Lidia tells Ana that she's going to sing a song by Shakira.

CLARE
(Remembering how Ana used to love Shakira) Shakira. Then what happened?

MARTY
They talk about Shakira until it's their turn to enter the holding room. Helen goes off to a corner to practice, and it's really boring waiting around, so Ana decides to come home. But then Lidia asks her to practice with her. She's really, really nervous. So, Ana stays.

CLARE
(Begins to text her friends) What song?

MARTY
I forget. An old one.
(ANA re-enters)
What song did Lidia sing?

ANA
"Gypsy"

CLARE
(Continues to text) "Gitana"! You used to love "Gitana".

ANA
(Holds up two tops) I can't decide.

LUISA
(Holds up one the tops from Colombia) Take this one. It goes well with jeans.

ANA
(Takes a look) No.

LUISA

But it's really cute. And it will make you stand out from all the other
girls.

ANA

I don't want to stand out. I just want to do it my way.

LUISA

Suit yourself. But don't forget, it's being Colombian that got you
noticed in the first place.

ANA

No, it's not.

LUISA

Yes, it is.

ANA

I got noticed because of my singing.

CLARE

But how? How did you get noticed?

ANA

We were practicing the song. First in English, then in Spanish.

LUISA

She'll *sing* in Spanish, but won't speak Spanish.

MARTY

And then one of the producers hears them, and asks Ana if she wants
to audition.

LUISA

Adopted teenager from Bogotá competes to become the next Canadian Idol. Gold. Pure Gold. Wait! Adopted teenager from Bogotá living with two mums! Even better!

CLARE

And you said yes?

ANA

No, I said no.

MARTY

So she asked Ana if she would sing a duet with Lidia.

CLARE

And you said yes?

ANA

No, I said no.

MARTY

But then Lidia begged her to say yes.

CLARE

So you said yes.

ANA

Yeah.

(CLARE texts furiously.)

CLARE

And you auditioned.

ANA

Yeah.

(CLARE texts furiously.)

CLARE

And they moved you onto the next round. This round.

ANA

Yeah.

(CLARE texts furiously.)

HARRIET

How many people are competing again?

ANA

Two hundred.

HARRIET

And how many get to go on TV?

ANA

Twenty.

CLARE

And the top twenty compete to be in the top ten. Then the top ten compete to become *(pause for dramatic effect)* the Canadian Idol!

(Luisa's phone vibrates in her pocket.)

LUISA

(She pulls it out and looks at it.) Anita's dropping by.

MARTY

What? Now? Why?

LUISA

She has a good luck present for Ana.

MARTY

(To ANA) It's really getting late. You need to finish packing.

HARRIET

How about socks? Do you have enough socks?

ANA

(Gets edgy) I don't know.

HARRIET

Clare, go upstairs and see how many pairs of clean socks she has in her drawer.
        (CLARE exits.)
(HARRIET calls after her) Without holes. *(To ANA)* If you don't have enough, I'll do a wash or buy you some and drop them off.

MARTY

Okay, back to tops.

LUISA

And then, accessories.

ANA

Accessories!

LUISA

Earrings, bracelets, belts.

ANA

Accessories!

HARRIET

We should have started packing way earlier.

MARTY

Okay. No need to panic. Tops, sneakers, accessories.

(ANITA enters.)

ANITA

Hello, hello, hello.

HARRIET/LUISA

Hi/*Hola* Anita.

(HARRIET waves, LUISA goes over to kiss ANITA on both cheeks.)

ANITA

Isn't this exciting?

ANA

I feel sick.

ANITA

I'm sure it's a few butterflies. That's all. I can't stay long. I just wanted to wish you luck and give you this.
(She hands ANA a large rhinestone brooch).
For a little flash.

MARTY

I'll say.

ANA

Thank you.

(CLARE enters with the socks and a box of makeup.)

CLARE

Seven.

HARRIET

Without holes?

CLARE

Without holes. *(Holds up the box)* What about makeup?

ANA

(Edgier) Makeup?! I forgot about makeup. Can't I go without any?

MARTY

Sure. Why not?

LUISA

You can't perform without any makeup.

ANITA

She's right. You need makeup.

ANA

This is getting too intense.

HARRIET

(Quick) Clare, pick out some makeup for Ana to take with her, and find something to put it in.

LUISA

I have a cloth bag from Bogotá. *(Beat)* If it's not too ethnic.

HARRIET

Perfect.

MARTY

Back to tops.

ANA

I can't do this.

HARRIET

Sure you can.

ANA

No, really. I can't. I can't do this.

(She exits.)

MARTY

(Looks at her watch) They want her checked in by 8:00. We need to leave in twenty minutes.

ANITA

I can drive her.

MARTY

(Abrupt) No. I mean, I'm going to drive her.

HARRIET

(Gets up) I'll go talk to her.

(ANA re-enters.)

ANA

(To HARRIET) I don't know what to do. I want to go and I don't want to go.

HARRIET

I know. But it will be fun! You'll have a good time.

ANA

I don't want to leave you.

HARRIET

I'm going to be fine. Anita will drive me to chemo. And I promise, I'll eat vegan.

ANA

Yeah. But I still don't want to leave.

HARRIET

Tell you what. You'll call me when you get to the hotel. And then, you'll call me again from your room once you've settled in. You'll hear my voice, and you'll know I'm okay. You can try it for one night, and see how it goes. You can call me as many times as you want. If you want to come home tomorrow, you'll come home.

MARTY

(Gets up) We've got fifteen minutes. Go choose your tops and sneakers. I'll pack them up and Luisa will add some earrings and bracelets.

HARRIET

Then, Marty will drive you down, and you'll call me when you get there. I'll be here. Waiting.

(Music is played to transition from Scene 5 to 6.)

Scene 6 Joy and Injustice

(HARRIET's kitchen. May. ANITA, LUISA, and HARRIET are having coffee.)

ANITA

(Indignant) So now you're saying I'm an unethical person.

LUISA

I didn't say that.

ANITA

Yes, you did.

LUISA

No, I didn't. I said that transnational adoption is a way of supplying wannabe parents in rich countries with children from poor countries. And –

ANITA

I'm unethical because I find homes for orphaned children.

LUISA

When poor parents have to send their children to an orphanage
because they can't take care of them, and then parents from rich
countries go to those countries to adopt those children because they
can afford to take care of them, then that's –

ANITA

Every child deserves a home.

LUISA

Every mother deserves to bring up her own children.

(HARRIET listens to LUISA stating her argument, with pride.)

ANITA

It's better for children to live in an orphanage than live with a
family?

LUISA

No. But –

ANITA

Yes or no? Living in a family is better than living in an orphanage.

LUISA

It's not only about –

ANITA

Yes or no? Your life here with Harriet is better than it would have
been if you had stayed in the orphanage?

LUISA

Yes.

ANITA

Yes or no? Adoption saves children from homelessness.

LUISA

Some children, yes, but –

ANITA

Yes or no? Adoption saves children from disability, from dying?

LUISA

Yes. But why do children from poor families need to be adopted to get medical care?

ANITA

I can't answer that question. Life's unfair. And I refuse to be blamed for all the injustices of the world.

LUISA

I'm not blaming you.

ANITA

I think overseas adoption is a fine way to make a family.

LUISA

But it comes with problems.

ANITA

All families have problems.

LUISA

Particular kinds of problems. Being separated from your biological family. Being sent somewhere far from home. Growing up in a family that's white, when you're not.

ANITA

You seem to be doing just fine.

LUISA

(To Harriet with affection) I've been lucky.

ANITA

So, maybe I'm not so unethical after all. I matched you up with Harriet.

LUISA

(To Harriet) Help me!

ANITA

You don't agree with her?!

HARRIET

I understand her argument.

ANITA

What argument? That you're unethical because you adopted her and Ana? Because you took them away from their "cultural roots"?

HARRIET

No. That sometimes adoption prevents social reform in poor countries.

ANITA

So, you regret adopting them?

HARRIET

No! Of course not. I can believe what Luisa says is true and not regret adopting them.

ANITA

And how does that work?

HARRIET

When I look at things up close, right in front of me, I have my own personal joy of living with Luisa and Ana. But when I move back, I can see the injustice of parents having to give up their children to keep them alive and healthy. The joy and the injustice live side-by-side.

ANITA

The injustice is that there are still too many children waiting for families. And that's something I can do something about.

LUISA

And, that there are still too many mothers dying of illnesses that they don't need to die from. That's something *I* can do something about.

HARRIET

And I'm very proud of your work.

LUISA

It's not only my work. It's Clare's work too! And your work, and Marty's work. *(With regret)* Everybody's, except Ana's.

HARRIET

Maybe one day …

(Luisa's phone vibrates in her pocket.)

LUISA

(She pulls it out and looks at it.) It's Jorge.

(She leaves the kitchen to take the call.)

HARRIET

So.

ANITA

So. What's the routine around chemo?

HARRIET
Ana drives me to the hospital and lets me out at the front door. I go in, she parks and meets me upstairs. But you can just drop me off and pick me up when I'm done.

ANITA
I want to stay and keep you company.

HARRIET
I'm really not very good company. And by the end of the day, I'm wasted. Really, really tired. It would be better if you just came to pick me up and poured me into the car.

ANITA
I wouldn't expect you to entertain me. I'd just sit there. With a book. But I'd be there to help you if you needed it. Ana says that you have to drag your IV with you to go to the bathroom. I could help.

HARRIET
That's okay. I'm used to dragging the IV.

ANITA
But I want to be there.

HARRIET
How about you come to visit on day five? The day after chemo, I feel I could throw up at any minute and spend most of the day on the couch. But by day three, I start walking around and by day five, I usually feel pretty close to normal again. Or if you wait until day six, we can go for walk somewhere.

ANITA
Are you sure you don't want me to stay with you in the hospital?

HARRIET
I'm sure.

ANITA

(Disappointed) Well, if you're sure.

HARRIET

I know this may not make sense to you, but it's easier for me to go through it alone.

ANITA

But Ana always stays with you.

HARRIET

Ana feels calmer if she stays with me. I know you'll be okay with dropping me off and picking me up.

ANITA

I just want to be a good friend.

HARRIET

(Takes her hand) Dropping me off and picking me up is being a good friend. It's what I want.

(Music is played to transition from Scene 6 to 7. HARRIET brings out a cardboard box and two children's books. She puts the box on top of the other boxes and puts in the books.)

Scene 7 Absent Impact

(Harriet's kitchen. June. There are now four boxes of children's books on stage. ANA is singing the last verse of "Absent Impact" *for CLARE.)*

CLARE

Well, I like it. I really like it. What's it called again?

ANA

"Absent Impact"

CLARE

"Absent Impact". Awesome. You should be proud of yourself.

ANA

Everyone keeps on telling me that.

CLARE

You made it to the top forty.

ANA

But I didn't make it to the top twenty.

CLARE

Neither did 180 other people.

ANA

Maybe I shouldn't have sung my own song.

CLARE

It's a great song. It tells a story. And it has a lot of feeling, a lot of emotion. It's deep.

ANA

You think?

CLARE

Oh, yeah. The only thing is –

(LUISA enters.)

LUISA

Play it from the beginning. I didn't hear the words.

ANA

You won't like it.

LUISA

How do you know?

ANA

I know.

LUISA

I want to hear it.

ANA

I'm telling you, you won't like it.

LUISA

(To CLARE) I'll like it, right?

CLARE

Yo no sé [I don't know]. *Quizas no te guste* [Maybe not].

LUISA

Why not?! *(To ANA)* Try me.

> *(ANA pauses for a moment, then begins to sing. CLARE becomes anxious.)*

Rusty yellow taxi
Took her far away.
I kept on looking back
Watched my mother's face
Until she couldn't see it anymore.
Blossom on the pavement
Kept on looking back
Heavy heart within on
Broken absent impact.

It was the last time I saw her face that day
It was the last time whoa oh uh oh
And all the laughter it drained from the house that day
It was the last time whoa uh oh
Annie, are you there?
I'm always looking out

For you, sister.

Blessed are the memories
Blessed were the days
Childish was the score
The universe was ours.
Dreams were made in cars
Our lovers cut from magazines
Faded teenage idol
Forefront of the fall
I cannot hear for silence
I wilt as you withdraw.

It was the last time I saw her face that day
It was the last time whoa, uh oh
And all the laughter it drained from the house that day
It was the last time whoa, uh oh
Annie, are you there?
I'm always looking out
For you, sister.

Think I hear you rushing through the back door
Treading muddy boots on the kitchen floor
Grooving on over to the radio
Dancing to the countdown on the Sunday Chart Show

It was the last time I saw her face that day
It was the last time whoa, uh oh
And all the laughter it drained from the house that day
It was the last time whoa, uh oh
Annie, are you there?
I'm always looking out
For you, sister.

You keep on running, running
You keep on running, running
You keep on running away.

You keep on running, running
You keep on running, running
You keep on running away.

You keep on running, running
You keep on running, running
You keep on running away.

                    LUISA
(Silent for a moment, then) It's about me.

                    ANA
Not just about you, about me too.

                    LUISA
You have no right to write about me without asking first.

                    ANA
It wasn't just –

                    LUISA
Do you want the whole world to know our business?

                    ANA
The –

                    LUISA
And going back to Bogotá to build a clinic is not running away.

                    ANA
Well, that's what it feels like.

                    LUISA
Harriet was fine while you were competing. *(To CLARE)* Wasn't
she?

CLARE

Yeah.

LUISA

She managed fine. And she'll manage fine while we're in Bogotá.

ANA

That was at the beginning of the regimen. It gets harder as you go along. Especially near the end.

LUISA

I know.

ANA

No, you don't. You weren't here last time. *(To CLARE)* You remember what it was like the last time.
        (CLARE nods.)
It was horrible. Tell her.

CLARE

It was very bad.

ANA

Tell her! Tell her how green Harriet's face was. How she didn't even look like herself. What she looked like without eyebrows. Tell her!

LUISA

It's only eight weeks.

ANA

Eight weeks is a long time.

LUISA

Harriet wants us to go. *(To CLARE) Verdad* [Right]?
        (CLARE nods.)
Dile [Tell her]. *(To ANA)* Clare asked her if she wanted her to stay home and she said no. She said just because she was having a lousy

summer, it didn't mean everyone else had to have one, too. Anyway, there's nothing we can do for her while she goes through chemo.

ANA

You can be here. So she has support on the really bad days.

LUISA

(Angry) Marty will be here.

ANA

(Also angry) Marty isn't her daughter.

LUISA

Marty is her wife! What's wrong with you?

ANA

What's wrong with *you*? Running away to Bogotá? Just when it's going to get really bad.

LUISA

(Furious) I'm not running away.

ANA

(Also furious) Did you ever think about me?

LUISA

(Surprised) What?

ANA

That I might need you here? So I don't have to go through this alone? So I don't feel abandoned?

LUISA

No one's abandoning you. You won't be alone. Marty is here. Anita is here.

ANA

I want you to stay. Both of you.

LUISA

It's been three years since I've been back. There are things I need to do. I'm going to look for our *Mama's* family. The records the Sisters have are already twelve-years-old. The longer I wait, the harder it will be to find them.

ANA

Please.

LUISA

I promised the Sisters we'd start building the clinic this summer. They're expecting me. They're expecting Clare. Everything's been arranged. I can't disappoint them.

ANA

They can start building without you. Someone else can do it. Someone who lives there.

LUISA

It's our project. We've fundraised for three years. I want to be there.

ANA

You can go next summer.

LUISA

There's no reason to wait for next summer. Harriet told us she's fine with us going this summer.

CLARE

I asked her. She said she wanted us to go. She said it was important for us to go.

ANA

What do you expect her to say? That it isn't important? Of course, it's important. But just because she said it was okay to go doesn't mean it's okay to go. What if … Have you ever thought … I mean, she might … Who knows if we'll have another summer with her?

CLARE

(Upset) Shut up. Don't say that.

ANA

It's the second time. How many people survive the second time?

CLARE

Lots of people. Lots of people survive.

LUISA

(To CLARE) Maybe you should stay.

CLARE

No. I want to go.

ANA

You *both* should stay. How are you going to feel if something happens and you're not here?

CLARE

What?

(CLARE starts to tear up.)

ANA

I'm not saying it will. But if it does. How are you going to feel?

LUISA

(Angry and upset) Terrible. We're going to feel terrible. How do you think we're going to feel? But we can't stop living just because Harriet has cancer. She adopted us for a reason. To give us a better

193

life. To give us a chance to make a difference back home. And that's what I need to do. Go back home and make a difference.

ANA

Just wait. Until the end of the summer. Until she's done chemo.

LUISA

(Upset, but firm) I can't. I've waited three years. I can't wait anymore.

ANA

Please.

CLARE

(Upset, resentful) Okay. Fine. I'll stay.

ANA

You'll stay?

CLARE

Yes.

ANA

(To LUISA) And you?

LUISA

I'm sorry. I have to go.

ANA

(Raises her voice) You don't *have* to go.

LUISA

(Raises her voice) I'm going.

(MARTY enters.)

MARTY

What's going on?

CLARE

(Very upset) Ana thinks Harriet might die and we shouldn't go to Bogotá. I'm going to stay, but Luisa's going.

LUISA

(To MARTY) No one's going to change my mind.

(LUISA exits.)

ANA

(Calls after her) That's because the only person you care about is yourself!

MARTY

How did all this get started?

CLARE

(Very upset) Ana's song.

ANA

She's the most selfish person in the world. I can't believe she's my sister.

(ANA exits.)

CLARE

(Explodes with disappointment) I wanted to go so much!

MARTY

(Comforts her) I know.

CLARE

(Crying) It's not fair. It's not fair I can't go.

MARTY

No, it's not fair.

CLARE

It's not fair that Harriet could die.

MARTY

(Crying too) No. It's not fair.

> *(Music is played to transition from Scene 7 to 8. HARRIET brings out a cardboard box and three children's books. She puts the box on top of the other boxes and puts in the books.)*

Scene 8 Date Night

> *(HARRIET's kitchen. June. MARTY enters carrying her books from school. HARRIET has lit some candles, and there are containers of take-out food on the island counter.)*

MARTY

(Puts her stuff down) What's all this?

HARRIET

Date night!

MARTY

Date night?!

HARRIET

BBQ ribs and ice-cream. I asked Anita to pick them up for me.

MARTY

We haven't had BBQ ribs since –

HARRIET

I know!

MARTY

(Looks around) Where's Ana?

HARRIET

Out.

MARTY

Out where?

HARRIET

At a movie with Clare. I told them we needed some quiet time to ourselves tonight.

MARTY

Wow. Ribs and ice-cream.

HARRIET

(Gives her an envelope) And a surprise. New York after chemo.

MARTY

(Opens the envelope) New York!

HARRIET

We've never been together.

MARTY

New York!

HARRIET

Central Park. Museums. Broadway. If we can't make it to Bogotá, we can make it to New York.

MARTY

You've had good day.

HARRIET

A really good day.

MARTY

New York. After chemo. *(Beat)* It's not too expensive?

HARRIET

It is expensive. But to hell with it.

MARTY

But we just bought all that audio equipment for Ana. There isn't much left in the savings account.

HARRIET

I know. I cashed a bond.

MARTY

You cashed a bond? From your RRSP?

HARRIET

New York. After chemo.

MARTY

It seems extravagant.

HARRIET

It is extravagant. But if not now, when?

(Music is played to transition from Scene 8 to 9).

Scene 9 Good-bye

(HARRIET's kitchen. June. LUISA's suitcases are by the door, ready to go. HARRIET and LUISA are saying goodbye.)

HARRIET

Are you sure you packed enough medical supplies?

LUISA

Yes.

HARRIET

Do you have enough aspirin?

LUISA

Yes.

HARRIET

Advil? Gravol?

LUISA

Yes.

HARRIET

Imodium?

LUISA

Yes.

HARRIET

Antibiotics! *(Anxious)* Did you go to the doctor and get a prescription for antibiotics?

LUISA

Yes, don't worry.

HARRIET

(Anxious) And you filled the prescription, right?

LUISA

Yes, I filled the prescription.

HARRIET

(Anxious) I didn't have a chance to check your medicine bag. I always check your medicine bag. A good mother would have checked your medicine bag.

LUISA

(Takes her hand) I checked it myself. And then Ana checked it. We never go anywhere without checking the medicine bag. You are a good mother.

HARRIET

Really?

LUISA

(Squeezes her hand) Of course.

HARRIET

Because sometimes I worry that I haven't been good enough. I mean, your life, Ana's life, Clare's life... They've been so complicated. I've made mistakes. Maybe I shouldn't have … maybe it would have been better …

LUISA

Not to adopt us?

HARRIET

I mean, I can't imagine my life without you. But maybe it would have been better for you.

LUISA

Maybe. Maybe not. But I can't imagine my life without you either.

HARRIET

(Moved) You know, I'm very proud of you. You've grown-up to be a real kick-ass woman.

LUISA

Like you. Who knows what would have happened if you hadn't adopted us.

HARRIET

You still would have been a kick-ass woman.

LUISA

But not the one I am now. *(Beat)* Thank you.

HARRIET

(Moved) So, you'll call once a week. Just like last time.

LUISA

Yes. Every Sunday.

HARRIET

And you'll let me know if you need any money.

LUISA

I won't need any money.

HARRIET

But if you do.

LUISA

I'll let you know.

HARRIET

I'll be thinking of you. Every day.

LUISA

And I'll be thinking of you. Every day. I'm just sorry …

HARRIET

Don't be sorry. You're doing exactly what you need to be doing. It's what I want you to do.

LUISA

I just wish that I wasn't leaving when …

HARRIET

Me too. But whenever you feel sad or bad about being away from home, I want you to remember that you're where you need to be and that there's nothing more I want in the world than for you to be where you need to be.

LUISA

Thank you.

HARRIET

So you're going to send us pictures, right?

LUISA

Yeah, of course.

HARRIET

I want to see it all. The hole in the ground. The cement being mixed up. The floor being laid, the walls going up. All of it.

LUISA

Right.

HARRIET

You won't forget.

LUISA

I won't forget.

HARRIET

Okay. Well, Marty's waiting.

LUISA

Yeah.

HARRIET

(Moves to hug her) I love you.

LUISA

I love you, too.

HARRIET

And I'll miss you.

LUISA

Me too.

(Music is played to transition from Scene 9 to 10.)

Scene 10 Nightmare

(HARRIET's kitchen. July. There are now five boxes of children's books on stage. MARTY and ANA are unpacking food ANITA has brought.)

MARTY

Thanks for all this.

ANITA

No problem. *(To ANA)* All the fruit and vegetables are organic.

MARTY

Thanks.

ANITA

(To ANA) Have you heard from Luisa?

ANA

Clare has.

ANITA

And?

ANA

They've finished the foundation of the clinic.

                        ANITA
That's exciting!
         (ANA shrugs.)
Has she started looking for your family?
         (ANA shrugs.)

                        ANITA
You don't know?

                         ANA
No.

                        ANITA
You don't want to know?

                         ANA
No.

                        ANITA
I see.

                         ANA
Do you think that makes me weird?

                       MARTY
(Definite) No. That doesn't make you weird.

                         ANA
Everybody thinks I should be interested in going back to Colombia to find my birth family. Or, that I should be interested in building the clinic. Like Luisa. But I'm not. It's her thing. Not mine.

                       MARTY
And that's fine. There are other ways you can support the clinic. You don't have to go there and build it.

ANA

And they think that when you go back to your birth country, you automatically fall in love with it, because it's the place where you really belong.

(MARTY is quiet.)

ANITA

(Also quiet, then) But that doesn't always happen.

ANA

No! When we went back to bring Luisa home, I didn't fall in love with Bogotá. I didn't even like it. It was noisy. It was poor. I didn't feel like I belonged there. I didn't feel like it was my real home. And when we went to visit the orphanage, I started imagining what would have happened to us if Harriet hadn't adopted us. It was terrifying. You know?

ANITA

Yes.

ANA

That happened to you?

ANITA

It happened to Joe. I wanted both the boys to go back. To experience life in Colombia. Compare different ways of life. They were both babies when we adopted them. David never wanted to go back. And I didn't push him. But I did push Joe to go. And he had a good time. He liked the food, the music, the sightseeing. But when we went to visit the orphanage, it was upsetting. He wanted to come home right away. He started having nightmares, and I cut the trip short. We came home.

ANA

I have nightmares too. Like last night. I was who I am now. The same age, the same person. But I didn't live here anymore. I lived in an orphanage. And it's like the orphanage Luisa and I lived in, but it's not. It's darker. It smells. It's musty. Damp. I'm washing dishes. There's a piano in the kitchen. But the cover is locked. I can't open it and I can't play it. I stop washing the dishes and try to pick open the lock. I can't. Then Harriet looks in at the door of the kitchen. I'm so happy to see her, because now I can stop washing dishes and go home with her. But instead of coming in, she's backing away from the door and getting ready to leave. Leaving me there. All by myself. Washing dishes. I scream at her. Come back. You forgot me! You're leaving without me! But she doesn't hear me. I'm alone in that damp, musty kitchen. Then I wake up. And I remind myself that I don't live in an orphanage. That I live here. And Harriet is asleep in the bedroom down the hall. And I feel better. Until I remember that Harriet's in the middle of chemo.

> *(MARTY goes over and gives ANA a hug. ANA hugs her back.)*

MARTY
(Breaks the hug) We'll all feel better once the chemo is over.

ANA
You think?

MARTY
Yeah.

ANA
But what if the chemo is the only thing that's keeping the cancer away?

MARTY
One step at a time. When the chemo's over, Harriet will have more energy. We'll be on the other side. We can go places, do things. It won't be so intense. Speaking of intense. Helen called again. For the third time. How come you don't call her back?

ANA

Because.

MARTY

Because why?

ANA

Because I know what she wants.

MARTY

Which is what?

ANA

To sing with her. At Free Times.

MARTY

(Excited) Really?

ANITA

What's Free Times?

ANA

It's a small café in Kensington Market. Helen's got a regular gig there for the rest of the summer.

MARTY

Do you want to do it?

ANA

(Anxious) I don't know. Maybe. But it means less time with Harriet. Who knows how much time we have with her?

ANITA

Don't say that. The doctors are very optimistic.

ANA

Doctors are always optimistic. They told us the chemo would work the first time.

MARTY

If you asked Harriet about this, what do you think she'd say?

ANA

Try it once or twice and see how it feels. If you don't like it, you don't have to do it anymore.

MARTY

Right.

ANA

And then she'd say, "Go perform and I'll come hear you sing".

(Music is played to transition from Scene 10 to 11. HARRIET brings out a cardboard box and one children's book. She puts the box on top of the other boxes and puts in the book.)

Scene 11 New Regimen

(HARRIET's kitchen. July. There are now six boxes of children's books on stage. HARRIET and ANITA are looking through the fifth box of children's books HARRIET's been collecting.)

ANITA

Where did you find all of these?

HARRIET

Book sales. And those discount bookstores. They're almost all in English, but Clare said she'd translate them.

ANITA

And you're going to ship all these boxes over to the orphanage?

HARRIET

We were planning to take them with us.

ANITA

It's cheaper to ship them.

HARRIET

(A little edgy) Yeah, but I want to bring them myself.

ANITA

If you ship them before you leave, then they'll be waiting for you when you get there.

HARRIET

It's risky. They might not make it.

ANITA

I've shipped lots of things. They always make it.

HARRIET

(Getting angry) Yeah, but this time they might not.

ANITA

(Surprised that this is becoming a big deal) I use a very good shipping company.

HARRIET

(Angry) I'm sure it's a great shipping company. But I want to take the boxes myself.

ANITA

(Backs off) Okay. Fine. You'll take them yourself.
        (HARRIET starts to rummage through the boxes.)
What are you looking for?

HARRIET

(Edgy) I bought a new book the other day, and I can't remember which box I put it in.

ANITA

I'll help you. What's it called?

HARRIET

(Thinks) Shit. I can't remember. *(Agitated)* I hate this.

(While HARRIET rummages through the boxes, ANITA begins another conversation but HARRIET isn't listening.)

ANITA

So, I have another family who's interested in adopting from Colombia and wants to talk to someone who's done it.

HARRIET

Yeah?

ANITA

So, of course, I thought of you.

HARRIET

Uh-huh.

ANITA

Can I set up a coffee date?

HARRIET

Yeah.

ANITA

Good. When's a good time?

HARRIET

A good time?

ANITA

When's a good time?

HARRIET

A good time for what?

ANITA

For a coffee date.

HARRIET

Coffee date?

ANITA

With the people – What's wrong?
   (HARRIET doesn't answer.)
Something's wrong. Tell me.

HARRIET

What's wrong is that I can't find that damn book.

ANITA

That's not what's wrong. What's wrong?

HARRIET

(Takes a breath) My oncologist called this morning.

ANITA

(Anxious) And?

HARRIET

She wants to change the regimen.

ANITA

What? Why?

> HARRIET

She thinks a new regimen would work better.

> ANITA

The chemo isn't working?

> HARRIET

No. You know how it is. Sometimes it's hit and miss. It takes a while to get it right. She thinks the new regimen will work better.

> ANITA

I don't believe this.

> HARRIET

I know. It feels surreal. But she says changing the regimen will make a difference.

> ANITA

You need a second opinion. *(Takes out her phone)* I know someone who's married to an excellent oncologist. I'm going to call her.

> HARRIET

No. I don't need a second opinion.

> ANITA

(Looks for the phone number on her phone) But there are so many kinds of treatments out there, and you need to know the benefits and risks of –

> HARRIET

I know all about the benefits and risks of this one. I'm good to go.

> ANITA

(Keeps looking) It can't hurt to get a second opinion.

HARRIET

(Takes the phone away). No. Just stop it. Listen. It takes time to get a second opinion. I don't want to start second-guessing my oncologist. I just want to get this over with.

ANITA

But what if there's something else out there that would actually work better?

HARRIET

(Angry) I've made my decision. And it's the right decision for me. Okay?

ANITA

(Hurt) Okay. Of course.

HARRIET

Okay.

(They are quiet for a moment.)

ANITA

What does Marty say?

HARRIET

I haven't told her yet. I need some time for it to sink in.

ANITA

What about the girls? You have to tell them too.

HARRIET

Yeah. But there's no rush, right? There's nothing they can do for me right now.

ANITA

It doesn't matter. They need to know. Luisa will want to come home.

HARRIET

It's too early for Luisa to come home. And I don't want Ana to change her mind about singing with Helen.

ANITA

I can be there you when you tell them. I can help Ana through this. I can help all three of them.

HARRIET

Hey, hey, hey. When I'm ready, Marty and I will tell them. And we'll take it on together. Like we did the first time. I know you want to help, but Marty's their second mother.

ANITA

(Chastised) Of course. I'm sorry.

HARRIET

It's okay. I appreciate your concern. I appreciate everything you've done to help out. Taking me to chemo, bringing over food.

ANITA

It's nothing, really.

HARRIET

It's not nothing. And I'm really glad that you talked to Ana about what happened to Joe in Colombia.

ANITA

You know about that?

HARRIET

Marty told me.

ANITA

She did?

HARRIET

Yeah. She said she it helped.

ANITA

Good. I'm glad.

HARRIET

It makes me feel better knowing that the girls have you to talk to, too. That it's not all on Marty.

ANITA

(Touched) I'm happy it helps.

HARRIET

There's one more thing.

ANITA

What?

HARRIET

I'm going to need to get stuff organized. And I can't even remember the name of the book I'm looking for. Will you help me? Get my affairs in order?

ANITA

(Upset) Yes, of course. But it's too early to worry about that now.

HARRIET

No. It's not. Yesterday I was listening to Ana rehearse. The song she was playing was so pretty, so moving, and I thought to myself, "It's going to be so exciting to see where she goes with this". And then I thought, "I'm probably not going to get see where she goes with this".

(Music is played to transition from Scene 11 to 12.)

Scene 12 Someone Else's Turn

(HARRIET's kitchen. July. There are still six boxes of children's books on stage. ANA is finishing making up a salad. All of a sudden, she becomes anxious. She puts down the knife and starts deep breathing to calm herself down. After several breaths, she feels calmer and picks up the salad bowl to put it into the fridge. As she moves the salad from the table to the fridge, her hands begin to shake and she drops the salad bowl. Salad spills all over the floor.)

ANA

Shit. Shit, shit, shit, shit. Fuck. Fuck, fuck, fuck.
> *(She picks up one of the salad servers that is on the counter and throws it across the stage.)*

I can't believe it. I can't fuckin' believe it.

(She screams in frustration and anger. Hearing the scream, MARTY enters.)

MARTY

What's wrong?

ANA

I just want it to stop. It just doesn't stop. It just keeps growing, and growing and growing.
> *(MARTY begins picking up the salad off the floor and putting it into the bowl.)*

No matter what I do, no matter how many salads I make, that fucking tumour just keeps growing. It won't stop. It won't go away. It's never going to go away. What's the use of even trying anymore? When everything you do is useless? Fucking useless?

MARTY

Not everything is useless.

ANA

Yes, it is. Everything is useless. The chemo is useless. Fucking useless.

MARTY

Just the first kind they tried. Just the first kind. We don't know about this new kind. This one might work.

ANA

Might. Might. What good is might?

MARTY

(Stands up, puts the bowl on the counter). Might is all we got.

ANA

I'd do anything to make it stop growing. Anything.

MARTY

I know. Me too.

ANA

Even stop singing. I'd stop singing, go back to school, and never sing again if that would make it stop growing.

MARTY

Well, fortunately that won't help.

ANA

I just want her to be well. I just want her to be around. To watch me grow up. I'm still just a kid. I need her here. She can't die, she just can't die. It's not fair. How many mothers does one kid have to lose? It's someone else's turn. Not mine. It's someone else's turn.

MARTY

I know.

(MARTY walks over to give ANA a hug. ANA pulls away.)

(Music is played to transition from Scene 12 to 13.)

Scene 13 It's A Start

(HARRIET's kitchen. July. There are still six boxes of children's books on stage. CLARE is closing the laptop, which she has just used to Skype Luisa. HARRIET enters hoping to speak to Luisa.)

HARRIET

Are you going to Skype Luisa?

CLARE

I just finished.

HARRIET

I missed it?

CLARE

Yeah.

HARRIET

Why didn't you wake me up?

CLARE

I knocked on your door. But you didn't answer. And I opened the door and tried to wake you up, but you were really sleeping deeply.

HARRIET

Shit. How is she?

CLARE

Good. The walls are up.

HARRIET

The walls are up! Is Jorge still there?

CLARE

Oh, yeah.

HARRIET

So that's working out.

CLARE

Oh, yeah.

HARRIET

I'm sorry you didn't get to go, too.

CLARE

I'll go next summer. Luisa's going to start a girl's first aid group. She wants me to get trained and run it. My Spanish is getting better and better. *Todo el mundo me lo dice* [Everybody says so].

HARRIET

(With mixed emotion) That sounds great.

CLARE

Y Jorge trabajará con los chicos [And Jorge's going to run the boy's group].

HARRIET

Jorge's going back too?

CLARE

Oh, yeah. And you and Marty will come too!

HARRIET

I'd love that.

CLARE

You need anything?

HARRIET

No. *(Beat)* Actually, yes.

CLARE

What?

HARRIET

I need to find a way to get Luisa and Ana to start talking to each other again.

CLARE

Good luck! It's been so long. Six weeks.

HARRIET

I know. But did you know that Ana's decided to donate the money she makes at Free Times to the clinic?

CLARE

No.

HARRIET

It's a start, right?

CLARE

Yeah.

HARRIET

And she's written a song about the orphanage.

CLARE

Really?

HARRIET

It's called "Chanting". Ask her to play it for you. And ask her if you can send it Luisa.

(Music is played to transition from Scene 13 to 14.)

Scene 14 Waiting

(Harriet's kitchen. July. There are still six boxes of children's books on stage. ANA is playing "Chanting" for CLARE.)

"Chanting"

Visit the classroom
Where I spent my first grade
Sit at my desk
In the row by the door

I hear the Sister call out my name
Like a voice on a wave
Rolling home to the shore

And I'm chanting the Lord's Prayer
I'm chanting, chanting
The feelings I felt there
Still dancing, dancing
I'm chanting the Lord's Prayer
I'm chanting, chanting
Chanting.

Opened my desk
See what I've left behind
Cracks in the wood
Etched out names, petty crimes

Touched like a splinter
Collision of time
I've so much to learn
Now I'm rewriting my own lines

And I'm chanting the Lord's Prayer
I'm chanting, chanting
The feelings I felt there

Still dancing, dancing
I'm chanting the Lord's Prayer.
I'm chanting, chanting
Chanting.

May the chanting oh oh
Be everlasting oh oh (repeat)

And I'm chanting the Lord's Prayer.
I'm chanting, chanting
The feelings I felt there.
Still dancing, dancing
I'm chanting the Lord's Prayer.
I'm chanting, chanting
The feelings I felt there.
Still dancing, dancing
I'm chanting. I'm chanting.

CLARE

Awesome! I love it! Especially the line "Now I'm rewriting my own lines". That's a great line.

ANA

Yeah. I like that line too.

CLARE

And the chorus is so catchy. *(Sings)* And I'm chanting the Lord's Prayer/ I'm chanting, chanting. The kids at the orphanage will love it. I bet no one's written a song about their orphanage before! *(Careful)* Can I send it to Luisa?

ANA

If you want to.

CLARE

(Careful) She says the Sisters all asked about you.

ANA

(A little edgy) Yeah? What did she say?

CLARE

That you were here, taking care of Harriet. And that you were writing songs and singing.

ANA

And what did they say?

CLARE

They thought it was awesome that you were taking care of Harriet, and they told me to tell you that they're praying for her.
    (ANA nods.)
Every little bit helps. Right?

ANA

I guess.

CLARE

Waiting is horrendous.

ANA

I know.

CLARE

You should write a song called *Waiting*.

ANA

Really.

    (They are quiet for a moment.)

CLARE

(Very careful) So, if I had some news about Luisa finding someone from your birth family, would you want to know about it?

ANA

She found someone?
        (CLARE nods.)
Who?

CLARE

Your mother's sister. Your aunt.

ANA

Really?

CLARE

Yeah.

ANA

Well, I'm happy for her. For Luisa, I mean, because it means something to her. But it doesn't mean anything to me.

CLARE

Okay. But I'm glad you know. It felt too weird not telling you. Can you sing *Chanting* again? I want to learn the words.

        (Music is played to transition from Scene 14 to 15.)

Scene 15 Next Summer

        (Harriet's kitchen. July. MARTY walks in find ANITA taping up and addressing one of the boxes of children's books on stage.)

MARTY

Hey. What's up?

ANITA

I'm getting these boxes ready to ship over to the orphanage.

MARTY

(Anxious, agitated) What? No!

ANITA

No?

MARTY

(Agitated) No!

ANITA

Why not?

MARTY

Because we're going to take them ourselves.

ANITA

When?

MARTY

Next summer.

ANITA

Next summer is a year away. The children could be using the books now.

MARTY

(Angry) I don't care.

ANITA

What?

MARTY

I mean, we want to bring them ourselves. Next summer.

ANITA

But it doesn't make sense to keep them –

MARTY

It makes sense to me. It makes sense to us.

ANITA

Harriet said I should ship them.

MARTY

And I'm telling you not to.
> *(Goes over to the box that ANITA has just taped and rips it open).*

We're going to take every one of those books with us. And we're going to buy more of them. Every month, we're going to fill up one more box, and then, next summer, we're going to bring every single one of those bloody boxes with us when we go back and visit the orphanage and the clinic that Luisa built. *(Beat)* These boxes just can't just disappear. Things can't just stop. Things can't just end.

(Music is played to transition from Scene 15 to 16.)

Scene 16 Long Beautiful Life

> *(Harriet's Kitchen. July. There are still six boxes of children's books on stage. ANA is working on/singing a new song called "Heaven". LUISA arrives from Colombia and approaches Ana hesitantly. ANA looks up, sees Luisa and stands up to embrace her. MARTY and CLARE enter. HARRIET is not on stage. It's uncertain if she is just resting or sleeping upstairs or if she has died. The last image on stage is of HARRIET's family all together in HARRIET's kitchen.)*

"Heaven"

Heaven see the beauty in you
Heaven see the beauty in me
Heaven how I feel it everywhere, everywhere

Heaven shone and gave us choice
Heaven smiled and gave us voice
Straight into the heart, heaven everywhere

And it's gonna be a long beautiful life
It's gonna be a long beautiful life

Heaven is the dust that lies
Heavy on this open page
Constantly the heart
Heaven everywhere

Heaven is a lingering stare
Shooting arrows in the air
Now I must declare
Heavens everywhere

And it's gonna be a long beautiful life
Heavens in your bones chapters in your eyes
It's gonna be a long beautiful life
It's gonna be a long beautiful life

All is with you
All is in you
Always with you

And it's gonna be a long beautiful life
Heavens in your bones chapters in your eyes
It's gonna be a long beautiful life
It's gonna be a long beautiful life

End of play

ACKNOWLEDGEMENTS

I want to thank and acknowledge the participants I interviewed for this project; the Social Sciences and Humanities Research Council of Canada, which funded the research for this script through its Standard Research Grant program; the Department of Curriculum, Teaching and Learning at the Ontario Institute for Studies in Education, University of Toronto for their institutional support of the project, and Jocelyn Wickett and the workshop team for their assistance in developing the script. I also want to acknowledge the writers and filmmakers of the texts I worked with in writing *Ana's Shadow*. Their perspectives appear in this script.

The songs "Absent Impact", "Chanting" and "Heaven" were composed by Chantelle Pike and Hannah Dean, two singer-songwriters from the United Kingdom, who worked with a set of ideas I had for Ana's songs. To hear these and other songs written by Chantelle and Hannah please visit www.myspace.com/eyesforgertrude.

BIBLIOGRAPHY

INTRODUCTION

Behar, R. (1995). Introduction: Out of exile. In R. Behar & D. Gordon (Eds.), *Women writing culture*. Berkeley: University of California Press.

Clifford, J. (1983). On ethnographic authority. *Representations, 1*, 118-146.

Clifford, J., & Marcus G. (Eds.). (1986). *Writing culture: The poetics and politics of ethnography*. Berkeley, CA: University of California Press.

Denzin, N. (2003). *Performance Ethnography: Critical pedagogy and the politics of culture*. Thousand Oaks, CA: Sage.

Goldstein, T. (2008). Performed ethnography: Possibilities, multiple commitments, and the pursuit of rigour. In K. Gallagher (Ed.), *The methodological dilemma: Critical, creative, and post-positivist approaches to qualitative research* (pp. 85-102). New York, NY: Routledge.

Goldstein, T. (2003). *Teaching and learning in a multilingual school: Choices, risks and dilemmas* (includes the performed ethnography *Hong Kong, Canada*). Lawrence Erlbaum Associates. With contributions by Gordon Pon and Judith Ngan.

Goldstein, T. (1997). *Two languages at work: Bilingual life on the production floor*. New York/Berlin: Mouton de Gruyter.

Kumashiro, Kevin. (2000). Toward a theory of anti-oppressive education. *Review of Educational Research, 70*(1), 25-53.

Leavy, P. (2008). *Method meets art: Arts-based research practice.* New York, NY: Guilford Publications.

Saldaña, J. (Ed.) (2005). *Ethnodrama: An anthology of reality theatre.* New York: Altamira Press.

ZERO TOLERANCE

Toronto District School Board. (2008). *The road to health: A final report on school safety.* Retrieved July 29, 2013 from http://www.schoolsafetypanel.com/finalReport.html.

LOST DAUGHTER

Abella, I. (1992, December 2). The prayer and hope of Toronto's Jewish community: Shalom. *The Toronto Star*, H1-H16.

Betcherman, L. (1975). *The Swastika and the Maple Leaf: Fascist movements in Canada in the thirties.* Toronto: Fitzhenry and Whiteside.

Boyer, B. (1985). *The Boardwalk Album: Memories of the beach.* Boston: The Boston Mills Press.

Campbell, M., & Myrolvold, B. (1988). *The beach in pictures 1793-1932.* Toronto: Toronto Public Library Board.

Gross, J. (1992). *Shylock.* London: Chatto & Windus.

Levitt, C., & Shaffir, W. (1987). *The riot at Christie Pits.* Toronto: Lester and Orpen Dennys.

Pressler, M. (2001). *Shylock's daughter.* New York: Phyllis Fogelman Books.

Rosenberg, L. (1993). *Canada's Jews: A social and economic study of Jews in Canada in the 1930s.* Montreal: McGill-Queen's University Press.

Shakespeare, W. (1596-98/1992). *The merchant of Venice.* Cambridge: Cambridge School of Shakespeare, Cambridge University Press.

Speisman, S. (1979). *The Jews of Toronto: A history to 1937.* Toronto: McClelland and Stewart.

Vigord, B. (1984). *The Jews in Canada.* St. John, NB: Canadian Historical Association.

ANA'S SHADOW

Bonkowski, B. (2005). *Jesse's world: A story of adoption and the global family.* Milsons Point, NSW (Sydney): Random House Australia.

Boluda, A. (Director/Producer) (2005). *Queer spawn.* New York/ Barcelona: Anna Boluda.

Butler, S., & Rosenblum, B. (1991). *Cancer in two voices.* Duluth, MN: Spinsters Ink.

Casper, V., & Schultz, S. (1999). *Gay parents/straight schools: Building communication and trust.* New York: Teacher's College Press.

Eng, D. L. (2003). Transnational adoption and queer diasporas. *Social Text, 21*(3), 1-37.

Eng, D. L. (2006). Political economies of passion: Transnational adoption and global studies. *Gender and Sexuality, 7*(1), 49-59.

Eng, D. L., & ShinheeH. (2006). Desegregating love, transnational adoption, racial reparation, and racial transitional objects. *Studies in Gender and Sexuality, 7*(2), 141-172.

Gray, K. M. (2009). *'Bananas, bastards and victims'?: Australian intercountry adoptees and cultural belonging.* Saarbrucken, Germany: VDM Verlag Dr. Muller.

Jacobson, H. (2008). *Culture keeping: White mothers, international adoption, and the negotiation of family difference.* Nashville: Vanderbilt University Press.

Kennedy, R. (2003). *Interracial intimacies: Sex, marriage, identity, and adoption.* New York: Pantheon.

Opper, N. (Director/Producer). (2009). *Off and running: An American coming of age story.* New York: Nicole Opper Productions.

Register, C. (2005). *Beyond good intentions: A mother reflects on raising internationally adopted children.* St. Paul, MN: Yeong and Yeong.

Trenka, J. J. (2005) *The language of blood.* St. Paul, MN: Borealis Books.

Trenka, J. J. (2009). *Fugitive visions: An adoptee's return to Korea.* St. Paul, MN: Borealis Books.

Trenka, J. J., Oparah, J. C., & Sun, Y. S. (Eds.). (2006). *Outsiders within: Writing on transracial adoption.* Cambridge: South End Press.

Turner Strong, P. (2001). To forget their tongue, their name, and their whole relation. In S. Franklin & S. McKinnon (Eds.), *Relative values: Reconfiguring kinship studies.* Durham and London: Duke University Press.

Vande Berg, L., & Trujillo, N. (2008). *Cancer and death: A love story in two voices.* Creskill, NJ: Hampton Press.

Vonk, E. (2001). Cultural competence for transracial adoptive parents. *Social Work*, *46*(3), 246-255.

CPSIA information can be obtained at www.ICGtesting.com
Printed in the USA
LVOW10s2247051113

359969LV00001B/5/P

9 789462 094505